**BST**

7/17/08

# THE
# Alpha Factor

# REVIEWS OF THE ALPHA FACTOR

Wes has nullified many theories that everyone has held to be true for decades! He has discovered the real levers for managing revenue growth.... no more intuition! While most of us are still trying to figure out who the customers really are, Wes has the model that finally determines what they really want! Opinion is determined by feeling and not intellect. Wes' factual intellect in this book has blown away many, perfectly well thought-out opinions!

*— Dan Cousino, Six Sigma Consultant*

The Alpha Factor is a must-read for anyone with responsibility for revenue-side success, not just CEOs and those who want to be CEOs.

This book is important to more than just CEOs and those who aspire to be CEOs. It should be read by every business unit manager, product or brand manager, and sales manager, as well.

*—Curt Neunighoff, United Pet Group, Spectrum Brands*

A powerful, influential book, "The Alpha Factor" unveils the mystery to achieve market dominance and makes the case that customer needs can really be known and met.

If you want more sales, more profits, more growth, then learn and apply the secrets of "The Alpha Factor".

*—Bud Handwerk, President, Annamar Associates, Inc.*

# T H E
# Alpha Factor
# P R O J E C T

*The secret to dominating*

*competitors and creating*

*self-sustaining success*

# Wes Ball

**Westlyn Publishing**
**Lititz, PA**

ISBN 978-0-9800031-0-9
Library of Congress Control Number: 2008921322

Cover and interior design by MDM Creative,
Lancaster, PA
Type composition by North Market Street Graphics, Lancaster, PA

**How to order:**

Single copies may be ordered through The Alpha Factor
website at www.thealphafactor.com.

Also visit The Alpha Factor website at www.thealphafactor.com

Thank you, Dan, for all the hours you spent with me at Starbucks in the early stages of writing this book, talking through what I was learning and helping me figure out what I was missing.

Thanks, Matt and Rem, for helping me make this understandable and for devoting so much time reviewing this, while you were both trying to start your own consulting businesses.

Most especially, thanks, Dad, for all the help you gave me in reading and re-reading this work as it progressed from little more than a brain-dump to something cohesive. But thanks even more for taking the time when I was young to teach me about business, marketing, and what success really looks like. I could never have done this without your immense wisdom and insight.

Finally, thanks, Lynn, my dear wife and best friend. You have stood by me through weakness and health, good times and bad, both when I spent far too much time with my company that kept me from focusing upon you and also when I was underfoot working at home. Your faith in me has inspired me to become better than I could have been without you.

# CONTENTS

Introduction - ix

## Section 1: *The Alpha Factor Project*

**Chapter 1:** The Alpha Factor Project - 3

**Chapter 2:** Where the Alpha Factor Exists - 15

## Section 2: *What Alphas Really Look Like and How They Work*

**Chapter 3:** The Secret of an Alpha - 47

**Chapter 4:** Alpha Assets—the Key to Managing Self-Sustaining Growth - 83

**Chapter 5:** Rules for Strategic Application of Alpha Learning - 116

**Chapter 6:** Spotting Potential Alphas - 136

CONTENTS

## Section 3: The Big "Ah-ha's"

### Big Ah-ha #1 - 153
*You don't have to be the biggest to dominate decisions in your category.*

### Big Ah-ha #2 - 156
*Price is the last decision criterion applied, not the first.*

### Big Ah-ha #3 - 160
*You don't have to be the first to market with an idea to be the dominant marketer of it.*

### Big Ah-ha #4 - 164
*You don't have to have the highest quality to be the dominant player.*

### Big Ah-ha #5 - 167
*Perceptions drive decisions—not the "hard" factors you believe might*

### Big Ah-ha #6 - 172
*You can predict who will grow dramatically before that growth even starts*

### Big Ah-ha #7 - 175
*Measuring final outcomes often blinds one to the causes that drive them.*

# CONTENTS

**Big Ah-ha #8** - 179
*Competition is desirable, because it can be
controlled to support you.*

**Big Ah-ha #9** - 184
*Don't follow the leader.*

**Big Ah-ha #10** - 187
*The customer decision process is extremely complex,
but it can be understood, quantified, and influenced.*

**Big Ah-ha #11** - 191
*You can manage the revenue side of the profit equation.*

**Big Ah-ha #12** - 193
*Dramatic shifts in market share can occur within short time
periods, even in well-established and
highly-competitive categories.*

**Big Ah-ha #13** - 195
*You can create a process for generating
self-sustaining success.*

**Big Ah-ha #14** - 199
*Innovation has to be more than new product
development or improved internal processes.*

**The Final Chapter:** Your Next Steps - 202

# INTRODUCTION

What corporate leader would not like to see his company become the Alpha of its product category, the dominant leader that everyone else follows, making it the controlling competitor in the category? What CEO would not like to know he also is building self-perpetuating success while maximizing growth short term? Most CEOs dream of having this kind of corporate influence and control. We all dream of having the ability to attract customers away from competitors without having to use price discounting to attract them; of having the leverage with distribution channels that means we don't have to worry as much about promoting our product because they would do it *for* us, believing it will make them wealthier than anything else they sell; of knowing that referral agents are regularly recommending our product because they believe so strongly in it; of controlling the decisions being made throughout our product category by customers, competitors, and distributors.

Through real-world experimentation over more than a

decade, I discovered that this isn't a dream. It's a reality that almost any company can achieve by understanding the secrets of the Alpha—that rare business that dominates decisions in its category and reaps the rewards of higher profitability, lower competitive pressure, and more control over its future and the future of others. These companies have been able to create such influence for themselves that almost everyone in their category looks at what they are doing before making strategic decisions of their own. And, instead of that following being a reason for concern, it is a point of competitive advantage because it gives them dominant control over what happens in their category.

My hope in writing this book is to help every CEO, every corporate employee who aspires to be CEO, and every financial analyst who watches businesses to be able to finally understand clearly what creates the potential for long-term self-sustaining profitable growth and market dominance. My research team discovered many surprises through the long-term research project, The Alpha Factor Project, that revealed these secrets. There were also many big "Ah-ha's" that helped us finally understand why the things we had learned in school didn't work as planned in the real world of business. We discovered the core secrets that many of the successful companies we studied and used to test theories did not even recognize in themselves as being the cause of their success.

I am going to share with you the secret of how almost

any company can grow dramatically, increasing profit and sales without discounting, and become a more dominant, influential player in its industry and product category. We proved that result by testing the secrets we discovered with real-world businesses and creating dramatic growth, even when none had occurred for that business in a decade or more.

Test these findings yourself and see whether you can't create growth beyond anything you've experienced before by using traditional methods.

*Wes Ball*

*Note: Although I have used the masculine pronoun for owners and CEOs throughout this book, it was done only for convenience and not as a slight to woman-owned and woman-managed businesses.*

# SECTION 1:
# THE ALPHA FACTOR
# PROJECT

# 1

## THE ALPHA FACTOR PROJECT

Every healthy organization has an Alpha—a leader who drives the vision, defines what it means to be in that organization, maintains order, and makes sure everyone is fed. Where a healthy, nurturing Alpha exists, everyone else in the organization follows and finds contentment in following. Where no Alpha exists, chaos reigns, and no one is content. The interesting thing is that this same dynamic extends outside of a business organization and into the marketplace itself, where an Alpha business can control what happens and who gets what.

Most people seem to want to believe that Alpha dominance applies only in the animal world. A long-term research study proved that it is also the secret to everything a CEO wants in the business world. This study, including more than 100,000 interviews and real-world tests of creating growth and sustainable success with more than 75 businesses of various sizes in more than 40 product categories, delved into the core causal factors that create Alpha dominance for a company in an industry or product category—the factors that almost any organization can use to give itself more control, stronger results, greater growth potential, and sustainable success.

Possibly the most intriguing finding of this long-term study was that it proved that almost any organization can manage the revenue generation side of its business to create better results than managing the cost side can accomplish.

Every strong business leader wishes that he could make his company the Alpha in its industry or product category. Being the Alpha means much more than just being the competitor with the greatest dollar share. It also means that the company has control over the expectations of its customers, the actions of its competitors, and the distribution of its product. Being the Alpha means that you have far more control over your company's future than do any of your competitors. It's not just about controlling costs to manage profit; it's more about having the influence over the revenue side to not have to worry as much about costs in order to drive strong, sustainable profits and growth.

The fact that every business leader wants to be an Alpha, yet so few have been able to achieve it even for short periods of time, is the reason this massive research project started. We wanted to discover what the real core causal factors were that drive growth and long-term success.

What we discovered along the way surprised us and the business leaders with whom we worked, because the causal factors often turned out not to be the ones that we or they had expected. Many of these factors were believed to be unmanageable, yet we discovered they could be influenced and managed far beyond anyone's expectations. Many executives continued on their way, shocked to discover that they could, in fact, manage and influence the revenue generation side of their business at least as much as they could the cost side. And the results were little short of astounding.

> *Our research was focused on discovering what the core causal factors were that drive growth and long-term success.*

For instance, U.S. Savings Bonds, a product of the U.S. Department of the Treasury since right after World War II, turned around a long-term double-digit decline to become the fastest-growing financial product in the United States. They didn't do it by offering rates higher than their competitors, which they believed would be the deciding factor, but, rather, they did it by employing a strategy that few would have predicted might create such fervor for a new, low-interest-rate financial product. Within just a few months of its introduction, a new U.S. Savings Bonds product, the I Bond, changed the perception of Savings Bonds among financial journalists from being "the worst financial product in the U.S." to being a "smart investment for smart investors." In less than six months, this new product was generating more than 2 million per week in online sales alone (not counting its other three distribution systems)—a number that any financial institution would love to achieve on an ongoing basis. The Treasury did it by learning how to help people discover what they really want as opposed to what they thought they needed to buy. The Treasury changed expectations to drive decisions its way—a key trait of an Alpha.

Subway Sandwiches and Salads was able to grow their second-toughest U.S. market from 11 to 67 franchises in less than a year and more than double per-store sales for stores that participated in the Alpha Factor Project learning. They did this while reducing discounting and without changing anything in their product mix, locations, or published pricing. They did it by learning how to make their products more valued just the way they are and learning how to make people want to help them succeed—key traits of an Alpha.

A regional food brand of a national food products marketer grew from a steady number four or number five in dollar share for the previous 12 years to triple their share and become the number one brand in their category in the region in just one selling season. The brand also did this while cutting discounting and without changing product, pricing, or distribution. In fact, they did it even though it had been proven in blind taste tests to be the worst-tasting product in its category. They did it by learning how to motivate their distributors to market their product for them at the expense of competitors and learning how to drive consumer expectations— all key Alpha traits that helped even this smaller brand succeed.

> *You don't have to be the Alpha leader of your industry or category in order to benefit from this learning.*

Armstrong World Industries, at that time clearly the Alpha among manufacturers of flooring, carpets, and ceilings for residential and commercial use, doubled sales of its leading brand of resilient floor tile without changing anything about the product, its pricing, its distribution, or its promotion other than to cut promotion costs by half and focus on a completely different motivation for influencing sales. The company did this by ignoring the pleas of its salespeople to discount more and give more away, recognizing instead who the real influencers of sales were and how to motivate them to be more influential—one way Alphas get others to do the work for them.

A regional personal injury attorney overtook all of his competitors in less than six months, including a very large, well-entrenched firm that had been the most visible and most-trusted one in the region until then. He did this by learning not to listen to those who said they knew how the legal business works and focusing instead on what really drives decisions—a critical method used by Alphas.

A vertical-market software manufacturer and marketer tripled its sales over the previous year in just one month without discounting, changing the product or its distribution, or even spending as much on advertising as its tough competitors. The software packages that it sold ranged in price from a $50,000 minimum to more than $200,000—at least as much and often more than competitive products. This company grew because it learned how to help buyers discover what they really wanted and how they wanted that delivered, so buyers recognized it in this marketer's product—a subtle method used by Alphas to overcome strong competitors.

These are the results of just a few of the more than 75 real-world labs used to test what we were learning in the Alpha Factor Project. We discovered that almost any company could grow both sales and profitability dramatically and sustainably using the learning from this research. You don't have to be the rare company that can actually become the Alpha leader of your industry or category in order to benefit from this learning; you can use this learning to grow, whether you are currently the top dog or just a small local player.

The Alpha Factor Project was a long-term research effort examining what creates sustainable success and dramatic growth. It looked at how customers really make decisions and define "value." It also looked for the common thread among those companies that clearly dominate their industry or category. Furthermore, it looked at the market dynamics that surround Alpha companies versus those surrounding product categories that have no Alpha, in order to understand both the processes and the results of Alpha leadership.

When I left the corporate world to start my own research and strategic consulting company, it was after I had worked in strategic marketing for one Fortune 100 and one Fortune 500 corporation. One of the long-term goals for me in starting this company was to understand what created success and how a corporate team could manage that to generate self-perpetuating success. One problem our team ran into right away in the initial observational stage was that there were so few true Alpha companies to observe. We weren't looking merely for companies that were leaders in volume, or sales, or customers. They had to be companies that clearly dominated market decisions and had clear control over the decisions being made by customers, competitors, distributors, and referral agents. It was obvious that some companies were the focus of almost all competitors in their category, but not all of them had the kind of overriding influence we were looking for. Compounding that was

> *The Alpha Factor Project looked at how customers really make decisions and define "value."*

the fact that not only were there very few, but those that existed were often in a downward slide from the influence they
had once held. And frequently the people in control of those
companies were not the ones who had helped create the original success and influence for the companies.

The second problem we ran into was that the individuals
who were directly involved with the success of an organization often could not tell us the real causes of that success. It
wasn't that they lied to us or tried to hide these factors from
us; rather, it was that they didn't actually know. They had
strong opinions based on their past experience and the opinions of many people around them, but when we did actual research into why customers were
buying from them the answers
given were dramatically different.
While we often heard from company heads about new products that
had changed everything or new
means of manufacture that allowed
lower costs or performance break-
throughs that had made the big difference, we heard very different things from the people who had decided to part with
their money to buy those things. It wasn't product, performance, price, availability, or any of the things that seemed to be
the obvious causes that created the demand. It was an entirely
different set of factors that were incidentally being addressed

> *We took some of the
> toughest challenges
> we could find
> to prove Alpha
> learning.*

by the innovation that had been achieved. Because those who created the innovation did not understand what it was that customers were actually buying, they found it extremely difficult to repeat that level of success with other innovations.

Because our study had to go beyond what was believed to be the causal factors in creating success, we decided that direct experimentation was the best method to follow. We used the hypotheses that had been developed in the early observational stage to create new growth for a broad range of companies, and then we did deep research into the causes of that success to understand what the actual drivers were. In many cases, we worked on the toughest examples we could imagine—companies that had not been able to grow in more than a decade yet had reasonably good products that we believed should be able to do better. This wasn't because of bad management or bad product; it was usually because the companies accepted the incorrect model of price, product, performance, and availability. In other cases, we were able to work with the leader of an industry who wanted to generate even more growth than previously. Through this process we were able to test and track what actually caused the success and what, if anything, sustained or diminished it over time.

In all, we used more that 100,000 interviews and more than 75 real businesses as test labs to achieve the final findings of the Alpha Factor Project. We knew we couldn't just sit around and ask each other what we thought was happening; we used proven statistical methodologies to determine what was going on. We learned which questions to ask in order to go beyond the obvious and uncover the real core motivations behind value judgments and purchase decisions. In the end, we were all surprised, not just with the model that we had uncovered but also with the results that came from using that model to create new growth and profit for real-world businesses.

> *Any business can create more growth without giving away profit.*

Most of what you will learn here contradicts much of what you have previously learned or been told. It is, however, the result of more than 15 years of research and testing to discover the real core elements that have created Alphas like Harley-Davidson, Coca-Cola, Mercedes-Benz, and Starbucks, and understand how to apply these elements to any company to create dramatic new growth.

The fact is that any business can create more growth for itself without having to give away profit—even against the toughest price-oriented competitors. This book will help you understand how you can accomplish that for yourself.

The implications of these findings are profound for business leaders. Few top managers today believe they can strategically manage the revenue side of their business. This study proved that they can. Few believe they can have control over their competitors through any means other than aggressive price promotion. This study proved that they can. Few believe that self-perpetuating, sustainable growth can be possible. This study proved that it can.

That's why the learning from the Alpha Factor Project is so important. It can change the way American business does business, generating more value for more people for more years. It can give corporate management more tools than cost-side management or product, price, promotion, and availability on the revenue side.

This learning can also change the way people invest, because it finally points to how to really evaluate a company's potential for success. This potential is not in the short-term, obvious factors that dominate investment analysis now, but, rather, in the amount of influence the company is able to wield in the marketplace and how it uses that to generate growth.

**This book was written for . . .**

**. . . anyone who is or wants to be CEO of** their company and who wants to understand how it is possible to manage and drive the revenue generation side of the company.

**. . . business unit executives** in leading corporations who want to understand not only how they can maintain their leading role but also how to think about innovation and growth so they can make themselves even more resistant to competition in the future.

**. . . executives in second- and third-tier companies** who want to understand how they can create more control, dominance, and price leverage for their companies.

**. . . owners of small to medium-size companies** who want to become dominators of smaller segments of the market, whether that market is geographic or categorical.

My hope is that this book will inspire more corporate leaders to take the steps needed to drive that kind of profitable growth. Our economy needs it as much as the stock market does. I believe that only through understanding what truly creates an Alpha can we hope to grow strong, healthy, sustainable companies through wiser investment strategies and to develop leaders who can create and sustain long-term revenue generation for years to come. This book can be the first step in driving that understanding.

# 2

## WHERE THE ALPHA FACTOR EXISTS

Ever since I entered the business world, I've heard analogies of dog packs or dogsled teams used to illustrate how businesses, markets, and competition work. As I discovered through the Alpha Factor Project, there are, in fact, many similarities between a healthy dog pack and a healthy product category. As part of the Alpha Factor Project, I did a lot of research into Alpha behavior in the animal world. I discovered a fascinating correlation and similarity between healthy, stable business categories and pack behavior, but it wasn't in the way that I have always heard it defined.

Alpha behavior is most typically described as the strongest male animal assuming power over the pack and then keeping that power through strength and intimidation. The entire pack then depends on this Alpha male for direction, and everyone else in the pack supposedly caters to him. The truth of Alpha behavior is, surprisingly, far more complex and far more applicable to business activities, especially when it comes to addressing competition.

True pack behavior is not (as it is all too often described) a jungle-type model, with the strongest and most intimidating always winning. Actually, a pack that operates like that cannot survive for long, and any Alpha that tries to lead using these techniques alone seldom lives very long, so the pack suffers. The Alpha's primary jobs are to help the pack find food and to manage the relationships within the pack. A healthy pack is highly organized, and that organization is managed by the Alpha.

> *True Alpha behavior is not a jungle-type model with the strongest and most intimidating always winning.*

Unlike the popular model, the Alpha is surprisingly compassionate and nurturing in how he accomplishes that task. What I learned as I observed pack behavior was that the core tool of the Alpha in getting and maintaining leadership is *influence,* not intimidation—he uses a large toolkit of techniques to create a desire among other pack members to follow his lead. He helps supply their needs, he encourages them when they need it, he demonstrates that he cares about them, he pushes them along when they need to be pushed, he forgives them when they ask for forgiveness, and he maintains an aloofness that makes others admire and want to follow him.

Actually, healthy parents do much the same thing for a child. They provide for his needs. They encourage him when he needs it. They demonstrate through a variety of methods that they care about him. They push him when he lags behind and needs a push. They forgive him when he is wise enough to ask for forgiveness. And they maintain a separation and aloofness that says, "We are your parents, and you should respect us." If they do not practice these things, their relationship with their child is precarious and the child is often uncontrollably rebellious.

The same is true for healthy businesses and product categories. Although most business leaders would love to be able to create fear in their competitors, that seldom happens through any legal means of doing business. Instead, as I will show you throughout this book, influence is the primary tool that creates followers, and it is the loss of that influence that leads to the loss of followers. That influence is created by a variety of activities that, just like those of the Alpha animal or the parent, makes those around him wish to follow his lead willingly.

In the business world, that activity of following behind an Alpha often gets lost in the confusion of competitive activities that are going on, but it is there. Figure 1 shows what a typical Alpha-controlled category looks like. Although it is not always as simple as depicted here, the process is consistent. The Alpha is the one driving expectations for the largest portion of

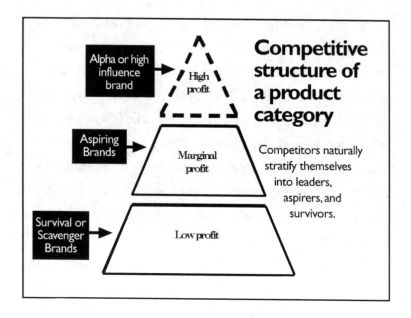

Alpha or high influence brand → High profit

Aspiring Brands → Marginal profit

Survival or Scavenger Brands → Low profit

**Competitive structure of a product category**

Competitors naturally stratify themselves into leaders, aspirers, and survivors.

the customers in the category, so most competitors are following the Alpha's lead. Distributors follow along, because they believe that the Alpha's control over customer expectations is advantageous to them, as do referral sources. What the Alpha does, others try to either mimic, make their own, or overcome by creating an alternative customer expectation.

In this type of product category, competitors become stratified into three groups: The Alpha is at the top (not necessarily in terms of sales or share, but in its influence over competitive decisions being made). A number of aspiring brands follow along behind it—they may be directly competing with the Alpha's offerings or trying to create their own alternatives that could drive customer expectations away from the Alpha. At the bottom are

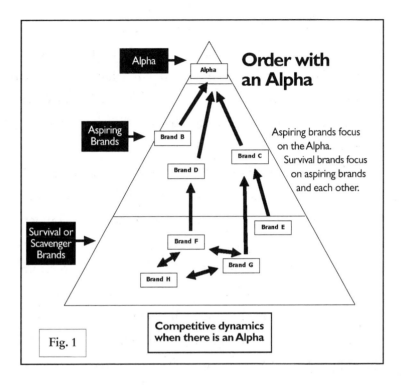

Fig. 1

**Competitive dynamics when there is an Alpha**

the survival or scavenger brands that scrap over whatever is left after the Alpha and aspiring brands get through. They are typically low-share, low-priced alternatives selling to small niche groups of people who don't believe that the better products offered by the aspiring brands are worth their investment. They often compete less with either the high-influence brands or the aspiring brands but more with each other for what's left over— that's why I refer to them as "scavenger" brands.

An example of this Alpha dynamic is the soft drinks category. Coca-Cola is the Alpha. What it does, everyone else tries to either duplicate or counter with something different. Pepsi is the chief aspiring brand (even though it almost gained Alpha status in the 1980s when it forced Coke to change its formula into New Coke, so it actually has what we could call super-aspiring brand status in this category—we'll discuss this phenomenon in more detail later). There are a myriad of other soft drink brands falling into both the aspiring and the survival brand strata, none of which have much impact on what Coca-Cola is doing, although they create the appearance of competition and activity. Some of them even provide unique quality offerings that have little impact on Coke or Pepsi but offer important options to customers.

Coca-Cola uses tremendously influential leverage with its retailers to maintain its dominance. Pepsi copies most of those techniques in an effort to maintain its distribution as well. The two of them have, however, left huge holes in the category where other brands can live and survive. Although Coke and Pepsi often have to consider the idea of eliminating all other competition, that would be both illegal and counterproductive. It is far better for them to have left holes for those smaller competitors to provide a spawning ground for new ideas and comfort for consumers who want to see other options that they may not wish to invest in producing. Many of these smaller companies become the innovators that can help the Alpha spot new trends it may have missed, allowing the Alpha company to use its leverage and influence to make the innovations without degrading its own influence by copying another leading brand.

In the Alpha-driven category, there may be several subsegments that allow other competitors to "rule" their own areas of influence, but the overall Alpha maintains the greatest control over the greatest part (or most profitable part) of the business in the category.

In the non-Alpha category, there is no one driving dominant expectations; therefore, product in the category is generally considered to be a "commodity"—that is, without much differentiation. Price battles reign and temporary dominance is held either through price, control of distribution, or other tactical methods. Figure 2 shows one of the typical ways a category without an Alpha works.

The packaged-cheese category is an example of this type of non-Alpha category. While Kraft dominates share in this category, dwarfing its nearest competitor in total volume, that strength is due mostly to distribution (meaning availability) and shelf presence (meaning you see more of their product on the shelves) rather than any driving of customer expectations. Kraft products merely fulfill a minimum need; they don't put everyone else on the defensive and create expectations among customers that drive decisions throughout the category. Customers feel little or no special satisfaction from buying Kraft cheeses, so except for a few isolated brands that have generated long-term emotional attachments with customers (for ex-

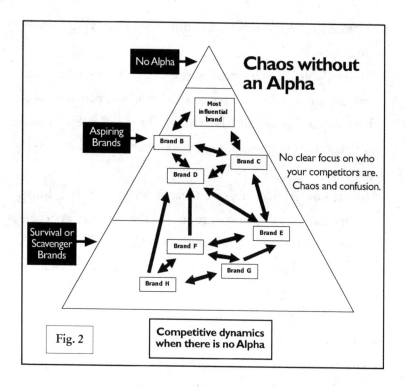

No Alpha → **Chaos without an Alpha**

Most influential brand

Aspiring Brands → Brand B

Brand C

No clear focus on who your competitors are. Chaos and confusion.

Brand D

Survival or Scavenger Brands →

Brand E

Brand F

Brand G

Brand H

Fig. 2

**Competitive dynamics when there is no Alpha**

ample, Velveeta), Kraft cheeses provide functional needs satisfaction at a reasonable price, but little else. Core loyalty to Kraft cheeses is low, and purchases are driven more by *lack* of knowledge of what might be better than by any real influence of the Kraft brand or its products.

We worked with a cheese manufacturer once who was so intimidated by Kraft's share dominance that the manufacturer assumed they could do little or nothing to grow their share against this giant. Once we showed them that expectations were not being driven by Kraft and that almost any cheese brand could grow significantly by starting to do so even in a small niche, the manufacturer suddenly started to see a different view of what their possibilities were. The company was able to refocus their innovation on ways to create new expectations in order to generate more influence for themselves and their brand with both consumers and retailers.

## FOUR CRITICAL SIMILARITIES BETWEEN THE PACK ALPHA AND THE BUSINESS ALPHA

---

### Similarity #1: The Alpha is looking forward and anticipating the needs of the pack.

---

The Alpha dog is not just "king"; he is also the visionary leader for the pack. One of his primary jobs is to find food for the pack. The business Alpha has the power to play the same role in his category. In fact, the Alpha defines what being in that product category is all about. Not only does he epitomize what the category represents, but he also has the power to shape the future of the category from his unique position.

This function of defining what it means to be in the category is the result of setting expectations. When customers, distributors, competitors, and referral agents see that what you are providing to customers is defining what is expected, they suddenly start pushing all of their decisions through that filter. They will drive their innovation toward addressing expectations similar to those of the Alpha.

This also puts the category Alpha in the leading role for innovation. As long as he continues to recognize the expectations he has defined and is addressing, not only can he continue to hold his Alpha position, he can also continue to drive new expectations for the category. Even if smaller competitors come up with interesting innovations that have the potential to drive expectations in a new direction, the Alpha has first choice at either "owning" that or rejecting it.

Sears was the clear Alpha in the general merchandise retailing category for the decades following World War II through the mid-1980s. They were the innovators in many product categories, but their real strength was in the comfort they gave customers who knew that if they went into a Sears store to buy hard goods (appliances, tools, and other "hard" items versus clothing, fashions, and "soft" items), they were going to get high quality at a great price (ranging from one of the lowest prices available anywhere to a Sears' Best product line that was equivalent to the best products available in the marketplace), with an unbeatable warranty. Every other general merchandise retailer followed their lead, because Sears had set the expectations for the category. No other retailers did what Sears did in terms of what they called Basic Buying—that is, creating lines of products and then having manufacturers make them to the defined specifications—but they certainly tried to compete on the same basic playing field that Sears had defined. It was only after Sears' management lost sight of what had made the company the Alpha that they lost control of the category and slid into their current also-ran position.

During their heyday, Sears led the industry in innovation—not just in retailing but in product development as well. Sears buyers and R&D teams often came up with fabulous innovations that were then produced by top manufacturers that often were not allowed to use those innovations on their own branded products. When I worked there, the dual-action agitator was developed for washing machines. That innovation was used in every washing machine that Whirlpool manufactured for Sears, yet Whirlpool was not allowed to use it themselves. They then had to create an alternative design that tried to approximate what the Sears product could do.

---

## Similarity #2: The Alpha makes sure the pack is fed.

---

As the leader of the pack, the Alpha animal is responsible for making sure every healthy pack member gets a bit of food.

He doesn't have to actually put it in front of the pack member, but if he hogs it all for himself and leaves nothing for the others, there will be an uprising.

This lead role in finding "food" is what has been called *primary marketing* in the business world—creating demand for the overall product category. As the leader that drives expectations, the Alpha business also has the responsibility to make sure that the overall category is attractive to customers. Those who abdicate that role find themselves being replaced by whoever does take the role, because that competitor becomes the expectation setter for the category. It only makes good business sense for the Alpha to take that lead role in generating demand; he will also be the one who reaps the greatest benefit.

I worked with the leading brand in a pet product category that was reluctant to take on the role of generating overall demand for the category. Even though the category needed to grow, there was a fear that anything they did that was not just competitively focused might generate more sales for competitors as well. This leading brand finally recognized that its hugely dominant customer share meant that no matter how much competitors received from their efforts, the lead brand still gained at least twice as much and also gained far more influence and control through those efforts. The end benefit to the Alpha is far beyond the investment made and far beyond anything a competitor happens to gain at the same time.

---

## Similarity #3: The Alpha helps define roles for other pack members.

---

The Alpha animal doesn't just sit at the top and fight off competitors. He more often is helping to define specific roles for members of the pack. Because he is concerned about the health of the pack, he takes an active part in defining useful roles for others. It typically starts with the process of natural selection, whereby the members of the pack find their own places in the pecking order. But from there, the Alpha seems to guide them into specific roles.

The business Alpha is able to do much the same thing. The Alpha can actually define niches for competitors by allowing them room to operate, rather than trying to eliminate them. The Alpha company doesn't use its influence to squash the competitors' efforts in that tightly defined area that it has left open to them, so the competitors stay there, comfortable with what they have. If the competitors try to step outside of that defined area, the Alpha has the influence and power to make it uncomfortable for them.

We already talked about the soft drink category. The ice cream category is another example of this. Ben & Jerry's made itself the Alpha of the ice cream category, not through trying to cover every base, but by defining a segment that drove expectations for the rest of the category and then allowing competitive brands to do whatever they wanted outside of their area. The very fact that they were so clever at defining their niche is what made it so costly for anyone else to enter it. Using flavor names like Chunky Monkey and Cherry Garcia and maintaining a funky, antiestablishment attitude were perfect tactics for a product category that had the potential to be an extreme self-indulgence for consumers. A study we did in the late 1990s showed that 80 percent of people who said they bought *only* the ice cream brand that was "on sale" admitted that they also bought Ben & Jerry's for themselves regularly, usually hiding it from other family members.) The bar they set for direct competition was so high that when others started adding similar flavors to their lines to compete with Ben & Jerry's success, it had no direct effect on Ben & Jerry's sales. In fact, Ben & Jerry's grew dramatically, while making other brands happy just to be competing in what they thought was a similar niche.

Ben & Jerry's has never gained the volume sales of Breyers or Edy's/Dreyer's, but they didn't care. They were far more profitable than either of those leading-share companies ever hoped to be, and they were essentially untouchable. If they had tried to take over the niches of those other brands, they would only have hurt themselves and the category as a whole.

---

## Similarity #4: Earned influence is the currency of the Alpha.

---

There are three primary forms of currency used in business:

1. Money
2. Relationships
3. Earned influence

Obviously, in animal packs money plays no role at all. Earned influence is the primary currency used to get what you want. Earned influence is the leverage you have to persuade others to do something because they *want* to do it for you. Earned influence is created by someone believing that you truly care for him and want the best for him. It can also be generated from a distance, when someone believes that you know or have something he doesn't, yet wishes he knew or had, and he believes you might be willing to allow him to have at least a piece of it.

The Alpha earns his influence by nurturing and providing for others. In the animal world, the Alpha points the way to food, safety, and prosperity for every pack member who follows his lead. In the business world, the Alpha points the way to increased revenue, sustainability of success, and prosperity for everyone who follows his lead.

---

Relationships play a very minor role in animal packs, except where mates or offspring are involved. In the business world, relationships are just a softer, and much less formidable, form of earned influence. Salespeople try to develop "relationships," because they believe that doing so will overcome new competitors that come along. But salespeople are continually being tripped up by new competitors that come in with more earned influence—companies that have proven in other places that they can point the way to more revenue, sustainable success, and prosperity. Relationships alone can't compete.

All too often in the business world, we reverse the order of this. We lose sight of the huge value of earned influence by placing money at the top of our list of value, with relationships second, and earned influence often a distant third. The fact is, however, that earned influence is the most valued currency available in the business world, just as it is in the pack. We just struggle with understanding how to create and sustain it sufficiently to make much use of it.

The problem with money is pretty obvious: It's hard to get, and once it's used, it's gone and has to be replaced with more hard work. Relationships are the primary currency of sales teams, although any sales rep can tell you how fragile they are in a world where people change jobs quickly and regularly, and they are often given big incentives (positive and negative) to avoid relationship entanglements. Sales teams have also been forced, in many cases, to use money as currency for getting what they want. For instance, in selling almost any item marketed through grocery stores, there is a high cost of entry, called a "slotting fee," that requires marketers to pay for the shelf space they will use in addition to being required to discount their products regularly for the benefit of the retailer.

Earned influence is the only currency that is increased the more it is used and, although it is hard to come by initially, it stays around long after the other two forms of business currency have disappeared through no fault of your own. Even after a person or organization has done something that undermines their earned influence, people will forgive them until it becomes quite apparent that something fundamental has changed that negates past earned influence.

Every politician knows the value of earned influence. Money comes and goes. Friendships wax and wane. But earned influence lasts until you personally undermine it or allow it to be undermined by someone else. Earned influence also supersedes money and relationships when the going gets tough.

Earned influence is the currency of Alphas. This is far more than just doing favors for people—that's relationship building. We're talking instead about making your organization look worthy of being trusted with someone's needs. Customers, distributors, and referral agents are looking for trustworthy organizations that can satisfy their needs, just as pack members will follow the animal most likely to lead them to food and make the pack successful. When a product or company proves that it can satisfy deep customer or distributor needs (meaning emotional, ego satisfaction needs), it gains a lot of earned influence. People start paying attention to it. Decisions start being made based on what the company's management says and does. And everyone, including competitors, starts following their lead.

Earned influence is the currency of the Alpha. It is what makes him able to lead without so much need for other forms of currency. In fact, we proved that a company that can develop earned influence (which can happen quite quickly once the company understands the real needs of the customers and distributors) can succeed even over seemingly stronger competitors that are spending many times as much money on marketing, advertising, and promotion. Money can't overcome earned influence.

## FOUR CRITICAL DIFFERENCES BETWEEN BUSINESS CATEGORIES AND DOG PACKS

### Difference #1: Not all product categories have an Alpha.

All animal packs have an Alpha—they could not survive without one. As soon as there is a vacuum created by losing the Alpha, a new one steps in. Many product categories, on the other hand, have no Alpha. There may be a category share leader, but that is not the same as having an Alpha.

As shown earlier in this chapter, the dynamics of a product category with an Alpha are significantly different from those of a category without one. The Alpha creates order and provides structure to the category, while the category without an Alpha is far more chaotic and driven by price promotion and infighting rather than by strategic expectations management.

Categories without an Alpha are also missing a great deal of their potential for profit generation. The value that is driven by an Alpha and the resulting hierarchy of price leverage that is created by the activity of competitors following the Alpha create more profit for more competitors. Prices and profitability usually are higher throughout the Alpha-driven category than in one where there is no Alpha. Total sales volume is also often higher in Alpha-driven categories than where an Alpha doesn't exist.

How many times have you heard business managers complain that there just isn't enough profit in their industry to make it worthwhile? That was exactly the situation in the ice cream category before Ben & Jerry's started to take the lead in setting expectations. Price was the primary driver of decisions among 70 to 80 percent of the consumers who bought ice cream. Since neither Breyers nor Edy's/Dreyer's was driving expectations as Ben & Jerry's entered the category, the impact was that suddenly there were more dollars being spent on ice cream (higher prices overall) and more profit was available to all marketers in the category. That doesn't mean that all ice cream marketers took advantage of that new potential. In fact, most continued to battle on price, while many others, including store brands, started raising prices and growing both their sales and their margins.

Product categories without an Alpha are sorry ones indeed. There is continual price battling, competitive maneuvering, promotional activity, and dissatisfaction among both the businesses in that category and their customers.

Banking is probably the best high-visibility example I can think of. No matter what changes in banking, there remains no Alpha. No bank has been able to define expectations, because they all work from the same playbook. In fact, that is exactly why credit unions have been so popular in many markets. They purposely use another playbook.

I'm not referring to the legal limitations placed upon banking institutions. I'm talking about the self-imposed limitations they hold on to so dearly. They steadfastly want to believe that they can't really show a caring attitude toward their customers—that might demonstrate a lack of professionalism or accuracy. They believe that they can't hint at any flexibility, although any business owner knows that banks are extremely flexible when they are finally forced to be as the alternative to losing an important account. Banks have a long list of "can't do's" that make it impossible for any of them to be an Alpha.

The result is that all banks seem pretty much the same in the eyes of customers. Few customers really trust their bank. And an average of somewhere between 25 and 50 percent of bank customers, especially on the business side, are one step away from going to someone else for their banking needs. If it weren't so painfully difficult to change accounts, there would be far more turmoil in the banking industry than there currently is—in fact, we discovered that the bank that can make customers believe they really care and that makes it easy to change banks can generate massive growth in a very short period of time. This doesn't require rate promotions, free toasters, or any other profit-reducing tactic. All it takes is making it easy for dissatisfied customers to say goodbye to the bank they believe has been thumbing its nose at them for years.

That's the result of not having an Alpha in the category.

---

## Difference #2: People are not animals.

---

Sure, this sounds too obvious to even mention, but the difference is significant. Animals seldom fool themselves into thinking that something that has not worked in the past might work in the future. People often do.

How many times do corporate leaders admit that they continue to try the same unworkable strategies over and over without predictable success? We have seen it all too often, and it's not just because they did not have the information to guide them in another direction. They frequently hold an overriding belief that their unworkable model *must* work and they just have to get it right, even though they have never seen any measurable, long-term correlation with success.

To pick the most obvious example of this: Many companies are totally committed to price promotion as a driver of long-term growth, even though the evidence is all too painfully obvious that short-term growth that is driven today by price promotion is undermined by losses in volume once the promotion is over. Usually, any simple measurement of average share shows no long-term gain, and profit almost always is lowered by using such tactics. Nevertheless, many companies are determined that price promotion is the way to success.

A consumer products company we worked with had been completely convinced that it had to do price promotion or its sales would completely dry up. This company demonstrated that the behavior of following the Alpha doesn't always occur even when there are highly visible successes, *if* the competitors in a product category are locked into a self-defeating model of how they believe things have to work—no matter how unsuccessful that model has been for them in the past.

The company I was working with was caught in a cycle of ups and downs based on when its retailers allowed the company to do price promotions, just like everyone else in the category. The company had never seen any net gain from this activity, but it believed that if it stopped it would surely slide backward. As we analyzed the consumer sales numbers, it was easy to see the temporary spikes in share that the price promotions were giving the company. But it was just as easy to see that in the weeks following the promotion's end, the company's share dropped dramatically so that the net average was right back to what the annual average share number had been for several years. All it seemed to have accomplished with those promotions was to reduce profitability during the promotional periods. The company argued, however, that the lower extreme of those swings could potentially be where it would end up if it stopped price promotion.

In the end, the company took a big risk and tested a different way to approach demand generation that included reducing the use of price promotion, raising prices, and focusing on creating new expectations among both consumers and retailers. The company's first experimental test market grew its share in that market by only 40 percent and increased profit by approximately 80 percent. A refined version was then used throughout the company's selling geography that resulted in more than double the share and close to triple the profit the company had been able to generate before. Because the company risked experimenting beyond what had not worked in the past, it discovered a whole new level of profitability and influence that launched it into a leading, rather than a scavenging, position.

At the same time, we watched the reaction from several key competitors to see what would happen, because the tactics we had used were visible to everyone and our fear was that everyone might jump on the bandwagon and copy what we had done. That would have forced us to move on to the next level of innovation to maintain the leading role. Not a single competitor changed its price promotion and other profit-reducing tactics despite the fact that they all clearly saw the strength that this company had suddenly been able to create for itself. I talked to a few competitors later to see what they were thinking. Not a single one had initially believed that what had worked *could* have worked, so they just kept on doing what they had been doing in the past. No matter what they heard or saw, they wanted to believe that this success was due to some hidden factor that they did not know rather than to the obvious one right in front of them.

---

## Difference #3: Change is undesired in animal packs— it is the key strategic tool in business.

---

Much of the effort of the Alpha in the wild is to maintain stasis so that the future is as predictable as possible. In the business world, change is one of the greatest strategic tools available to marketers. It's how you *use* change rather than how you

WHERE THE ALPHA FACTOR EXISTS

*react* to it that defines your current and future positions in the marketplace. Many companies try to make their future more predictable, but they accomplish that through methods that limit their success rather than maximizing it.

I worked with a large national bank whose managers wanted desperately to be able to predict success—not in terms of increased potential or increased market leverage, but rather in specific dollar outcomes they could expect from promotional efforts. They finally recognized that their efforts only limited their outcomes, because in order to be able to accurately predict an outcome, you must take away any unpredictable factors that might make you go over or under your projections. They wisely abandoned that in favor of increasing their potential for profitable growth.

Top-level packaged-foods marketers use an interesting form of this. Because much of their budgeting for a new product introduction requires knowing how much product to manufacture, they have a complex formula they use based on consumer reactions to the product in controlled research environments that dictates how much they should make and send to stores. The problem is that the formula they use is based on very specific introductory promotions that actually undermine the product's long-term success. That's part of the reason that the average percentage of new introductions among food products that stay on the shelves for more than a year is less than 10 percent—even though all those products passed through extensive research before they were ever considered for introduction.

The real trick in business is creating change that forces others to follow your lead. Any business has the potential to create greater influence for itself by instigating change. It is how smaller companies wedge their way into a position of more influence and greater sales. It is also how the Alpha keeps all of its followers following rather than striking out on their own and potentially creating a truly competitive new position for themselves. Change forces a reaction from competitors who are following. It can also, if used strategically, drive new expectations among customers, suppliers, distributors, and referral sources. When used in this way, it perpetuates success by making you the one with all the control over expectations and others the ones who must follow your lead or fail.

One of the things we noticed about new Alphas (meaning ones who had recently made themselves Alphas and, therefore, still had the individuals who created that success on the management team) was that they were comfortable with change and actually liked instigating it. Ben & Jerry's, Victoria's Secret, Microsoft, and Intel are all relatively recent Alphas. Each one thrives on change and uses it to keep competitors, customers, and distributors in line. In the cases of Microsoft and Intel, this strategy also keeps referral agents on the edge of their seats waiting to hear what's new.

I was fascinated to learn, for instance, that Intel has already developed at least two future generations of processors. They have already driven software development that will require these new processors. Everything is just waiting until the right time to introduce them. That leaves competitors in a constant game of catch-up rather than stimulating innovation that might threaten Intel's leading role.

The way smaller competitors have typically used change to create growth for themselves is through innovation that drives new expectations away from whatever the leading share brands offer. Honda wasn't even a serious factor in U.S. automotive markets in the 1970s. The first cars it introduced into the United States looked more like peanuts with wheels than any real car that an American might drive. But Honda used the fear created by the gas crisis in the late 1970s and in-novation that addressed hidden desires that Detroit's au-tomakers hadn't believed were worth considering to become an influential powerhouse with profitability and price lever-age that dwarfed anything Detroit had ever dreamed of. They created change in order to drive expectations away from the status quo. Both GM and Ford could easily have stepped on those efforts and made them their own, reinforcing their Alpha status in U.S. markets. Instead, they held to their old model that had just been outmoded by a small upstart, and they were left behind.

---

## Difference #4: There can be multiple Alphas
## in a product category.

---

Unlike animal packs where multiple Alphas cannot exist for long, there can be multiple Alphas within product categories. Continuing with the Ben & Jerry's example, while Breyers was the Alpha of premium ice cream (12 percent butterfat) for some time, Ben & Jerry's became the Alpha of the superpremium ice cream subcategory (14 percent + butterfat). Ben & Jerry's had no designs on the premium ice cream category. The overall category could have been sustained with two Alphas. Since Breyers lost their Alpha status and really lost their way, the influence that Ben & Jerry's created actually spilled over into the premium category, making them the Alpha for the entire category. Almost all products started following the innovating lead of Ben & Jerry's, while Breyers became an also-ran.

As marketers have known for a long time, segmentation of the market can be a powerful strategy for creating new opportunities. Looking at subgroups of customers or of customer needs often reveals significant new opportunities for innovation and growth. When this is combined with knowledge about Alpha behavior and ways to create a following within that sub-category, it can be one of the most powerful tools available for small or new competitors to become Alphas on their own. If managed well in a category that does not already have a clear Alpha driving expectations for the overall category, this could lead to a smaller brand becoming the Alpha for the overall category. Such a position doesn't guarantee that they will gain the greatest share in the category immediately, but it will make them significantly more profitable through increased price leverage and it will give them control over the direction of the category so they can define the future for themselves and their competitors.

That's what Ben & Jerry's did. They drove expectations in the superpremium ice cream subcategory in a way that affected expectations for the overall category, making them the overall category Alpha—not in size, but in influence, which made their profitability something others could only dream about.

## SUMMARY

Becoming the Alpha and sustaining your company as such in your category requires that you drive expectations and create earned influence. It doesn't require huge investments of capital. It doesn't take a great deal of time in most cases. It can occur even where there is an Alpha already existing, and you don't have to be or become the biggest in your category to become and remain the Alpha, gaining the benefits of greater profitability and greater control over your future and that of the category as a whole.

It does take a willingness to look beyond the playbook that everyone in your category is using and find the opportunities that change the way customers, competitors, distributors, and referral agents look at the category. By doing so, you will redefine what it means to be in the category and you will become the primary influencer of decisions from the top to the bottom of the competitive strata.

# SECTION 2:
# WHAT ALPHAS REALLY LOOK LIKE AND HOW THEY WORK

# 3

# THE SECRET OF AN ALPHA

There is so much bad information being passed along about what makes a great and successful business that it is hard to look past it to find the truth. This was one of the biggest hurdles our Alpha Factor Project research had to overcome. Many of the responses we got from interviewing business owners and corporate executives proved to be secondary factors in their success, not primary ones. That was not because they were lying but because they were using a filter that let them see only how they believed things worked rather than really recognizing what was driving success. They were getting their information through salespeople, distributors, employees, outside observers, and consumers, all of whom had their own views on how they *wanted* to believe things work. Some of those information sources also had ulterior motives for guiding perceptions one way or another, such as retailers (and often internal sales staff) who want marketers to believe that price is everything simply so the retailer can be a hero by offering the lowest price for a top-quality product.

Both top executives and second tier executives with line responsibility often stumbled over the same issues. We quite often heard things like "We're the biggest," "Our distribution is the strongest and most loyal in the industry," "Our quality is the highest among all competitive products," or "Our cost structure is among the best in the industry." More often than not, our research for them into the real drivers of customer decisions told a very different story. Many corporate leaders did not realize the hidden strengths they had that were actually driving success. In many cases, the strategic decisions they were making based on their mistaken belief about what created their success were actually undermining those critical strengths and hurting their long-term potential for growth and profitability.

> *Many corporate leaders did not realize the hidden strengths that were actually driving their success.*

## QUALITY AND PERFORMANCE ARE NOT PRIMARY DRIVERS

One of the most common errors our research revealed was the role of quality and product performance in creating a real edge in the marketplace. Neither quality nor performance proved to be a critical driver of decisions—rather both were merely proofs used by customers to rationalize and explain the decisions they had made in terms that they believed would make sense to someone else. Instead, there were much deeper emotional factors that were driving those decisions, and quality and product performance, at best, only helped prove what they believed at a more emotional level.

For much of the past three decades, Harley-Davidson motorcycles has been one of the most desired products in the world, yet few would claim that their quality and performance are anywhere near those of Japanese motorcycles. McDonald's quality has never been up to the level of many of its competitors, although McDonald's executives would

> *Many corporate managers have invested millions into increasing quality rather than what would really drive demand.*

probably fiercely argue that. Most fashion clothes that people pay exorbitant prices to wear would not be considered top quality. Even Mercedes-Benz, which has based much of its competitive advantage on the quality of "German engineering," has proven to have significant weaknesses in that area. Yet each of these brands can demand premium prices and each drives expectations for much, if not *all*, of its category. Despite that, many corporate managers have invested millions of dollars and significant effort into increasing the quality of their product rather than focusing on what would really drive demand.

It's not that customers would not prefer some rational way to make a decision based on performance and/or quality. This would certainly help satisfy the logical side of their brain—even though that side can be and often is easily overridden by emotional desires. Thus, customers tend to rely on a combination of emotional needs overriding rational ones and, in many cases, a lack of information useful for making logical product comparisons.

There is no doubt that quality and product performance could be primary drivers of decisions in ideal situations, if they strategically pointed to and proved a compelling emotional desire. In far too many situations today, especially at the retail levels where multiple brands are being compared, the information customers need to make such judgments is not available. Figuring out which of several products to buy is often more of a guessing game than a real decision process, because so little useful information is made available to the customers making the decision. Compounding that, customers seldom trust the critics and evaluators who are available, as we discovered. Customers are actually more inclined to trust their friends and neighbors than anyone who actually knows something about a product's performance characteristics.

Sears is one of the few companies that actually succeeded in using quality and product performance as strong elements of the decision process. Before they lost their Alpha status and became "Brand Central," they sold their own brands exclusively. They had complete control over what customers saw at the retail level and how the differentiation among products was communicated. Trust in Sears' brands was extremely high as a result of the effort they made to help customers feel comfortable by giving them logical trade-up information as well as by providing customer protection through some of the strongest warranties in the industry—ranging from "Satisfaction Guaranteed or Your Money Back" to free replacement forever for any Craftsman hand tool. The reliability of their products (at least in "hard" lines, like appliances and tools) had been proven good through years of performance, but that only helped customers feel comfortable enough to make Sears the first place they shopped for such products. By making sure that there was clear information provided about why one product was better than another and giving them a safety net of "satisfaction guaranteed," the decision became a lot easier for customers—and customers repaid Sears for that with strong loyalty.

> *Trust builds loyalty.*
>
> *Loyalty leads to recommendations.*
>
> *Recommendations lead to influence.*
>
> *And influence makes others follow your lead.*

But just looking at that loses sight of the real core drivers of decisions to shop at Sears. Sears did this so well that there was little or no need for any comparison outside of a Sears store. Trust was created because shoppers knew they had a choice among, at least, good, better, or best (and sometimes even more options were offered). The trade-up was logical and was based on both features (promising performance advantages) and aesthetics (at least in appliances). Each item in the line had a product information tag listing the features and benefits. Customers trusted Sears as the place where they were sure they could get a product that would perform well at a reasonable price, with no risk. That made people feel smart. They also typically felt appreciated, because Sears did a great job of conveying that to customers through everything from the way they were greeted and helped on the sales floor to how liberal the store's credit policies were. Sears was among the first to offer credit to newly married couples in the years following World War II, before the era of credit cards.

Contrast that with the typical retail shopping experience we all have to put up with today: A broad range of products is offered, with no logical differentiation that justifies the range of prices being demanded. We find few, if any, salespeople who know anything about a given product or are willing to help. Many customers leave the store feeling not only unappreciated, but also not very smart for having shopped there.

The point here is that a reputation for product performance or quality, and providing enough information to recognize this, provides a level of confidence that generates trust. Trust builds loyalty. Loyalty leads to recommendations. Recommendations lead to influence. And influence makes others follow your lead. Sears became and sustained itself for decades as the Alpha of general merchandise retailing because it made all other general merchandise retailers follow their lead by enabling customers to feel smart and appreciated. After Sears lost sight of its real strengths, those who took over the lead position in retailing never accomplished that to the level of Sears.

Harley-Davidson, on the other hand, has a very different set of drivers for its success. They certainly had to improve the quality and performance of their products before they could take the lead in the touring motorcycles market, but the company has never really gone far beyond simply addressing the minimum functional performance level required of a motorcycle. Instead, Harley-Davidsons have become among the most desired items in the world because of the personal significance that is acquired when you buy one.

I've seen meek men become confident and strong just by riding a Harley. I've seen women begin to feel that they are competition for any man by riding a Harley. Harley-Davidson motorcycles are not and probably never will be the best-made, best-engineered motorcycles in the world. They don't need to be. They can charge more than almost anyone else simply by providing owners with an aura of power that nothing else seems to provide.

Quality and performance are obviously important components of decisions, but only as they either meet minimum expectations or prove other, deeper emotional factors that truly drive decisions.

## PRICE IS NOT A PRIMARY DRIVER

Price advantage was another reason executives often cited for a company's success, although it was not the primary reason given by most top executives. It was disconcerting, however, that it was by far the most common answer given by national sales managers. They typically believed that their price advantage was what made them strong.

Those executives who believed that success was being driven by price were typically stunned when the research we subsequently did on the real drivers of purchase decisions for their and their competitors' products showed that price was one of the *least* important drivers, even among distributors who regularly intimidated marketers into believing price was critical. In the cases where we were able to help them translate the findings of our research into strategic implementation, they were astounded at the growth that could be achieved by moving away from price as the revenue generation strategy. In most cases, they were able to raise their prices *and* grow sales at the same time, compounding the impact on their profitability.

Through all our research, we never discovered an Alpha that had the lowest-priced product or that had become the Alpha as a result of having the lowest prices available. In fact, we never found a leading marketer in any category that actually had the lowest prices available among all the competitors in their category. Even Wal-Mart—known as the beast of retailing because its prices are supposedly so low that no one can compete with them, thereby putting small retailers out of business—does not price merchandise as low as many of their discount competitors. Wal-Mart is not the lowest price provider; they

> *Price was one of the* least *important drivers of decisions.*

have just made themselves appear to be that in order to attract customers away from any competitor. The real advantage Wal-Mart has is that, like Sears when it was the Alpha of general merchandise retailing, people trust them. You can return almost anything to Wal-Mart without questions being asked. You believe you are going to get a good product at a great price. You typically get a fairly good selection (although nowhere near the selection you could get from many other stores). And it's close to being a one-stop shopping experience. Wal-Mart drives expectations among customers of mainstream name-brand products by making people believe that you don't need to shop anywhere else.

People who shop at Wal-Mart feel smart, because they believe they are saving money and still getting a good product with minimal risk. And they are made to feel appreciated by pleasant greeters and easy return policies. Wal-Mart's ability to generate a following among customers, competitors, and referral sources is not based on price but on a set of highly emotional factors that make people trust them and make them the first choice for shopping in many product categories. In fact, one of the things that has always fascinated me about Wal-Mart is that, although they are recognized as having customers at the lower end of the demographic scale, in reality many highly educated, high-income consumers shop there regularly because they feel silly paying more for something at another store when a Wal-Mart is just as convenient for purchasing a functional product.

It is probably important to talk about another side of this price issue: couponing and promotional discounting. Almost all consumer products and distributors have long believed that couponing and promotional discounting are imperative for driving trial of product, which then can lead to loyalty. The truth is far different.

We did a long-term study of couponing and promotional discounting to discover the real impact they had on purchases. From our experience with consumer products, we fully expected to see at least trial of product being strongly affected by such tactics. Instead, we found that there was a hard-core group of people who try to buy whatever is on sale or whatever they have a coupon for. These are the people who go to the grocery store with boxes of coupons filed in order so they can easily find them. These represent about 10 percent of the population, and they have little or no loyalty to brands or specific products.

There is another 10 to 15 percent who never use coupons for any reason, although many still take advantage of promotional discounts on brands they already know they want. The other 75 percent of customers use coupons or take advantage of promotional discounts mostly for items they planned to purchase at regular price. This means that of those people who use coupons, 88 percent were most likely to use them for items they would have paid full price for. The other 12 percent would probably never become loyal customers. This constitutes profit needlessly lost to those marketers. Even where the discount or coupon was the deciding factor between two items customers considered essentially the same, we discovered that the discount given would have been better spent creating some positive differentiation for the product rather than just buying the customer for a single purchase.

The findings about trial of new products were even more disconcerting. As marketers have known for decades, there is a small group of "first adopters" who like to try new things just because they want to be forerunners. They don't need discounts or coupons to drive trial. In fact, they are often willing to pay a high premium just to be the first to have something interesting. The segment of the population fitting this profile changes by product category, but it is typically between 25 and 30 percent. Then there are those who wait to hear from someone else about the quality of a new product before buying it themselves. This segment represents about half of all customers out there. This leaves only about 25 percent who said that they might be influenced to try something new by a discount or coupon. In reality, however, their actual buying habits did not reflect that. More typically, they also simply waited to hear that something was a great product before taking the risk and trying it.

> *Reducing discounting and couponing grew profit, overall sales, and customer loyalty.*

That's not to imply that Alphas don't use couponing or discounting. They most certainly do—not because they really have to, but because they, like most marketers, have come to believe that it is what must be done to drive demand and to keep your distribution channels happy. In more cases than not, however, that approach has created more damage than benefit.

We worked with many organizations that initially believed promotional discounting and couponing were the secret to driving loyalty and growth. In every case, we were able to show them that they could dramatically grow not just their profit but also their overall sales and customer loyalty by reducing the amount of discounting and couponing they were doing.

Subway Sandwiches and Salads is a good example. Like most quick-serve restaurants and retailers in general, they struggled with this issue. They believed so strongly in promotional discounting and couponing that they even instituted a "loyalty-generation" program for ailing Subway stores that included high levels of discounting, which eventually dropped off over a period of many weeks. The idea was to start people off with buy-one-get-one-free offers to drive trial. The theory was that, as customers decided they liked the product, smaller and smaller discounts would be required until they would eventually no longer need discounting to keep them.

In reality , this program created a lot of discount-addicted new customers who left as soon as the offers disappeared. It was successful only in attracting that bargain-seeking fringe of the population, who felt cheated when they were eventually expected to pay full price.

## MANAGEMENT IS NOT A PRIMARY DRIVER— BUT IT IS A SUPPORTING FACTOR

Many executives pointed to an even more elusive factor as the cause of their success: great management—although they usually didn't use those exact words and the ways they defined it were almost as varied as the number of interviews we did. "Great management" was often intended to include things like cost management, management of stock price, visionary leadership, an understanding of marketing, and other concepts that are equally diffi-cult to correlate quantifiably with real, measurable success.

> *Where traditional management factors really had value was in* **sustaining** *growth, not in creating it.*

Certainly, these management concepts were revealed in many of the leading companies we studied, but we proved that we could take companies that demonstrated few or none of those things and still create dramatic growth for them using a completely different set of factors as the drivers of that growth. Often this resulted in the company becoming the leader in its category in a very short period of time, in spite of the fact that it had struggled to maintain a secondary or ter-tiary position before. These companies were able to realize all but the longest-term benefits of being an Alpha without nec-essarily having all of the factors traditionally identified as con-stituting "great management."

Where those management factors really played out was in *sustaining* the growth that was created, because without them, these companies often felt so uncomfortable in their new leadership position that they subconsciously under-mined their own success to get back to a more comfortable lower level.

# RELATIONSHIP IS NOT A PRIMARY DRIVER

The final commonly cited cause of success was something executives called "relationship" with their customers. They typically believed that they created that relationship through regular communications with their customers and, quite often, special VIP offers. Such things often proved to have minor impact because they helped reinforce some sense of appreciation; however, we discovered that customers don't really *want* a relationship with a product or a company. What they want most is some sense of deep satisfaction and significance. They want to feel smart about themselves. They want others to feel envious of them for being able to buy a particular product or for being smart enough to know it was the right product to buy. And they want to feel appreciated by the company in return for putting their trust in it.

## THE REAL DRIVERS

It all goes back to Maslow's hierarchy of needs. However, there is a subtle but important difference between overall life behaviors and how purchasing decisions are made.

Figure 3 shows the traditional hierarchy of needs introduced by Abraham Maslow in 1954, which I have simplified into three master categories. Maslow's theory held that a person must address safety and security before he is able or willing to address

Fig. 3

**Maslow's Hierarchy of Needs (simplified)**

personal satisfaction or significance. Therefore, a person will make decisions in order of what he most needs, shown by moving up the pyramid. He will seldom, if ever, address significance if he has safety or security issues facing him. The weakness in this theory is that every person, except where an immediate life-endangering threat exists, will actually act on his need for significance above anything else. And in a society where true life-threatening danger or starvation is experienced by few, people live mostly in the satisfaction and significance zones.

In terms of purchase decisions (Figure 4), where we are talking about decisions involving disposable income, we are typically vaulted into the realms beyond safety and security. It

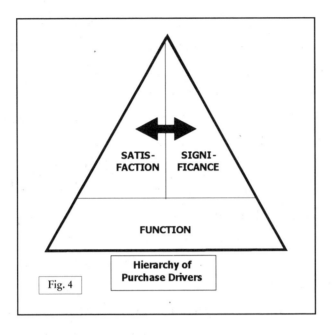

Fig. 4

**Hierarchy of Purchase Drivers**

is only in situations concerning trauma health care and self-protection that the safety/security issue typically biases decisions. In most cases, the decision becomes a matter of satisfying first the functional needs that the product is supposed to satisfy and then moving directly to the personal satisfaction and significance levels.

A car must be able to move and get a person from place to place. Depending on the need, it may also have to carry more than two people, have certain safety or convenience features, provide a certain range of fuel economy, and so on. Once these functional criteria are satisfied, the customer's personal satisfaction and significance concerns take a lead in the decision process.

Color, leather seats, convertible versus hardtop, and the like, are on the satisfaction side. Significance comes into play when customers start to take into account how others will think of them for driving a particular car. I hate to admit that my dissatisfaction with my Mustang Cobra started when I realized that those most enamored with the car were 10- to 14-year-old boys, not the people I really wanted to impress. I received more ego strokes driving the Mustang GT I had previously owned than I did with my Cobra, which cost a lot more than the GT. The primarily reason for this was that Ford had not made the Cobra brand mean anything to younger or even middle-aged Ford buyers the way it had when the "Shelby" name was attached to it.

Function (product performance and quality) is important only up to the point that the product doesn't meet minimum functional needs. The key is to address minimal functional requirements and maximum emotional ones (satisfaction and significance). On the satisfaction side are assessments like "I feel good using this product" or "I feel smart buying this product over competitive products." On the significance side are assessments like, "I feel appreciated by the company that makes this product" and "I believe others admire me for being able to buy this product." People want personal satisfaction from using a product—which can be in the form of feeling smart or experiencing something pleasing. They also want personal significance—to be more attractive to others, to be admired by others, or to be considered smarter than others.

One area of emotional significance that almost universally causes problems for businesses is customer service. This is an aspect of performance that almost every company measures in some way, in an attempt to understand why they are not generating more loyalty and customer satisfaction. The problem here is twofold: Customers aren't telling you the real reason for their dissatisfaction, and the term "customer service" invariably seems to be misunderstood.

First, when customers complain about customer service, the complaint was almost always initiated by a performance or quality issue. The product doesn't meet minimum functional performance—it doesn't work as expected, the information provided doesn't help, a bill seemed to be wrong—something didn't happen as expected, and the customer felt the need to contact the company. When we push through the real core issues driving low scores for a company on customer service, there is almost always a "below minimum" performance issue that could have solved it before it started. Often the highest scores for customer service go to suppliers that have not even had an opportunity to provide much customer service. Little or nothing has gone wrong to create the need for it.

*The problem is . . . customers aren't telling you the real reason for their dissatisfaction.*

However, when a customer service interaction is needed (and that is almost inevitable), we discovered that far too few customers walked away feeling appreciated and significant, even if the problem was solved. On the other hand, we heard of situations where customers actually thanked customer service reps for their help despite the fact that the problem was never solved. The difference was that the customer came away feeling significant and appreciated.

This is an area where both Alphas and non-Alphas struggle. Although there have been much discussion and training applied to improving customer service over the past three decades, little has actually improved, according to customers.

Microsoft is clearly the Alpha in the computer software category. They have created the influence to drive most decisions among PC users, yet (unlike the majority of Alphas, who are among the most admired companies) they are also one of the most disliked companies in America, mostly due to their customer service. Product performance typically creates the need for the contact, but the contact itself is enough to convince customers that they wish they didn't have to work with them. Try calling to get help on any given day, and you could wait on hold for 30 minutes or more (we were on hold for more than 45 minutes once, while we waited for someone to take our call to solve a desperate problem). Using the Internet to get help (Microsoft's way of reducing wait times) often gets you little or no help at all. Then you have to endure another day of trying to get an answer, losing hope that the problem will ever get solved. Personally, I have never had a single problem solved by

Microsoft, despite having issues that were causing terrible problems at critical times in a project. I just had to find my own way around them, including having to completely rebuild my hard drive right in the middle of a major project.

The primary problem might be the product's performance, the information available, or the expectations of the customer, but the customer service that ensues once this happens does nothing to overcome the already negative emotional response that is building. Instead, the interaction creates an even stronger belief that the customer is neither appreciated nor significant in the eyes of Microsoft.

Microsoft is the only Alpha we found that has maintained its position despite being so vehemently disliked. The thing that seems to keep customers on board is the perceived pain they would incur by making a transition to another platform. I have often wondered what would happen to Microsoft if that pain of transition disappeared.

## MANAGING THE CUSTOMER DECISION PROCESS

Alphas manage the customer decision process in ways that non-Alphas don't, to the same extent. Most exciting about this discovery is that almost any company that uses these Alpha techniques can dramatically change its status and success in the marketplace.

Probably the first thing we recognized was that Alpha control happens on the revenue side, not the cost side. Managing costs in order to create price advantage, as we have already seen, can have some small effect, but it is not a critical driver and often stands in the way of real growth opportunities. Managing quality and product performance have supporting effects, but they are not the factors that actually drive success.

Much of the problem for top-level executives in addressing revenue generation has been that there is little to help top executives understand how to manage the revenue side. Business schools certainly aren't providing much practical guidance. And business publications provide very little useful insight into how success innovations occurred or whether those innovations were truly the cause of success or the result of it.

> *Alpha control happens on the revenue side, not the cost side.*

Apple's success with the introduction of the iPod and the iPhone did not just occur because they were breakthrough, proprietary technologies (which is a debatable assumption right off the bat). I would argue that many other companies could have marketed those same technologies and not had the same success. I would argue that it was the work Steve Jobs and his strategic team have done to become the standard bearer for the simplicity-seeking, youthful technology crowd that made it possible for Apple to gain the quick acceptance of their product, as well as demanding such a high price for it.

On the other hand, when the Blackberry (a telephone, PDA, and Internet access device) was introduced, there were no lines of people waiting all night for stores to open, even though this product constituted a greater conceptual breakthrough. Yet introduction of the iPhone created such demand that hundreds of people camped out in front of retailers just to be the first to get one at a price higher than that of the Blackberry. Apple had done such a great job of managing revenue-side (demand) factors for a long period of time that there was a ready customer group just waiting for the product.

How do you manage something that is almost totally under the control of influences outside of your company? This requires far more than advertising and creative communications. They may play an important supporting role, but they cannot overcome a lack of foundational support in factors that truly lead to the creation of market demand.

For most managers, the purchasing habits of customers and distributors are seen as irrational and beyond much direct control, except at the basest levels of manipulative attraction (price, sexual attraction, fear, etc.). The reality of the Alphas, however, is that they maintain a great deal of influence (which equates to a high level of control) over the revenue side without having to resort to base-level attraction. As we have already seen, higher-level self-perception and personal significance provide far more long-term value than momentary appeal through lower-level attractors.

We discovered that many older Alphas did not even recognize the influence they have, how they got it, and how it can be used. Coca-Cola certainly did not recognize the influence they had when they decided to introduce New Coke and dropped their traditional formula. It was their customers who demanded the return of what is now called Classic Coke that saved the company from allowing Pepsi to take over as Alpha. Yet, I recall reading a statement by the CEO of Coca-Cola at the time, who said that the company's real business was to create value for stockholders. If that was truly the focus of the company's efforts, then it would not be so impervious to even disastrous internal decisions. Their real strength has been in managing drivers of decisions in ways that even internal management seems to have forgotten that they do.

*Managing costs to create price advantage can have a small effect, but it often stands in the way of real growth opportunities.*

This has to be painful to the many top executives who have invested so much in cost-side management, believing that it will drive real long-term value for their companies to the exclusion of investing first and wisely in revenue-side management. The truth is that you can't influence customers and distributors and referral agents who can drive growth for your company just by being more effective in controlling costs, except in a temporary and ultimately self-destructive way. Addressing costs only sets the stage for the need to lower costs again and again, while creating greater price leverage that allows costs to rise generates an expectation that higher and higher prices can provide greater benefits—and that's true at all levels of the marketplace, from customers to distributors to referral agents to investors. If you focus on cutting the cost side without managing the revenue side more wisely, you create a downward spiral that has killed and is killing many previously strong companies throughout the world.

> *There are so few Alphas around today, because most focused on cost-side factors rather than real drivers of self-sustaining success.*

That's why there are so few Alphas around today. Most of them lost their way by focusing on cost, product performance, quality, and other internal cost-side factors to the exclusion of understanding and managing the revenue side. Sears, Armstrong, Ford Motor Company, General Motors, Cadillac, Kmart, Snapple, Ben & Jerry's (they are still marginally an Alpha but are losing that position quickly), Softsoap, Woolworth, Caterpillar, Howard Johnson, Good Humor, Duesenberg, and Breyers are just a small sampling of past Alphas who lost their way by not managing the revenue side in the way they once had. In most cases, their cost side was managed well—or *too* well. They missed the most important factor in becoming and staying an Alpha: It happens on the revenue side by managing the customer decision process.

The management of the customer decision processes starts at the category level. Alphas define what it means to be in their particular category. Their example creates a vision for what you should expect from a product in that category.

> *Alphas define what it means to be in that category.*

John Deere became an Alpha by defining what farm tractors, and then lawn and garden tractors, are supposed to be. They set the standard for what you should expect from a tractor. Interestingly, the competition they have experienced from both foreign and domestic companies in recent years has been in the form of redefining what a high-quality tractor is and looks like. In the lawn and garden tractor market for instance, the real competition has not been from the lower-priced products that tried to fill in behind John Deere but from the high-end tractors that have redefined what a first-rate lawn and garden tractor is—something that John Deere "owned" for many years. Cub Cadet has started showing up in more and more high-end neighborhoods, where John Deere used to dominate. Cub Cadet has done that by making their product into the standard by which everyone else should measure a lawn and garden tractor. Similar things have happened with farm tractors, where high-end competitors are redefining what a farmer should aspire to own.

Any company wishing to become an Alpha must create a new, more inspiring vision of what it is to be in that category. It can't just follow the lead of someone else's vision. Ben & Jerry's redefined what you should expect to get in a superpremium ice cream—not just more fat, but lots more goodies loaded into it. Victoria's Secret redefined a socially-acceptable way to be "sexy." Coca-Cola redefined social refreshment beverages (yes, that was generations ago, but they blew away Dr Pepper, Pepsi, and a myriad of other brands at the time). Sears redefined what you could expect from a general merchandise retailer—Sears customers knew that Sears had already searched out the best solutions and then had them manufactured to their exacting specifications at a reasonable price. Armstrong flooring redefined the level of decorating help that you could expect from a home improvement products company—starting in 1918 they made themselves known for providing great decorating ideas in their advertising that made people look to them for ways to make their homes more elegant and attractive.

Note that none of these companies was first in its category. What each of them did was redefine what it meant to be in that category. They redefined expectations, making themselves the visionary leaders so that everyone else had to follow them.

For a company's management to engineer that kind of leadership control, quite often the vision for a category must be changed dramatically from being a "commodity" category (where there is little differentiation and heavy price competition) to being a category of self-satisfaction and personal significance creation for customers. To be effective in creating a vision that has this kind of longevity, the CEO of an aspiring Alpha must be continually asking his strategic team to understand what the key drivers of decisions are in the category (and for their proprietary products) and how those differ from what *could* be driving decisions to create more profit and growth for the company and the entire category.

> *You must understand the current key drivers of decisions and how they differ from what* **could** *be driving decisions.*

This is a difficult concept to grasp, but understanding it provides critical clues to how you can both *strategically* and *tactically* manage such a dramatic change in your category and for your company. Let's start with current drivers of decisions, as opposed to possible ones.

## IDENTIFYING DESIRED DRIVERS OF DECISIONS

Current drivers of decisions are obviously those that are currently at work. They are the set of reasons behind the decisions people are making today when they buy a product in your category. Desired drivers are those that customers wish were at work in your category—the ones that will address the higher-level emotional needs of satisfaction and significance.

It's important to know that *actual* current drivers are not the same as *stated* current drivers, because, as covered earlier, many times people can't or won't tell you why they are actually making decisions. People will often give you rationalizations that justify what they feel led them to the decision—these are things they believe you will understand and not question too closely, because emotional reasons are often hard to support if questioned. That's why so much research into the drivers of decisions concludes that price is the primary driver. It's the easiest thing to say when someone wants you to explain why their product wasn't purchased. It's also the one thing that almost everyone (except a really well-trained salesperson) will accept as a valid reason. In banking, "convenience" is one of those universally stated drivers of decisions. Few people think to challenge that concept with a justification of why all the other banks that were also "convenient" to the person were not chosen.

> *People can't or won't tell you why they are actually making decisions.*

Stated drivers of decisions are not the same as the real drivers of decisions behind the rationalizations. It's imperative to get to the real, emotional self-satisfaction and personal significance factors that underlie the decisions being made. If you can't find them, you are probably looking at a product or category that has not created expectations of higher-level drivers of decisions.

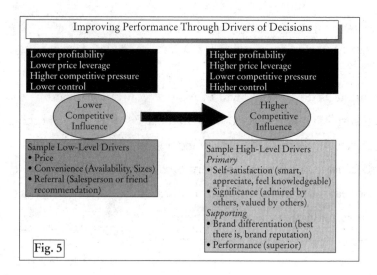

Figure 5 shows the difference between high-level and low-level drivers of decisions. High-level drivers of decisions can be at work in any product category, if an Alpha (or a company aspiring to become Alpha) has created higher expectations. High-level drivers create price leverage and increased profitability, lower competitive pressure, and greater control for the company and its brands. Low-level drivers of decisions reduce price leverage and profitability (to the point of creating price wars to survive), higher competitive pressure, and less control over decisions in the category and the company's future. At the low end of the scale is less influence, which creates greater vulnerability and less profit. At the high end is greater influence, which creates less vulnerability and greater profit.

The key to understanding this is that customers desire to

use higher-level drivers of decisions, not low-level ones. Customers want to be making decisions that positively impact their self-satisfaction and personal significance. It's only when no one has made such drivers available to them that they slip into lower-level ones, such as price, or convenience, or referrals and recommendations. If high-level drivers are available, they will seek you out.

Make it possible for customers to feel smarter, bolder, braver, more influential, more knowledgeable, more admired, or more fulfilled, and customers will flock to your product . . . at least as long as it meets the minimum functional requirements. As noted earlier, sometimes those functional requirements have to increase to be perceived as competitive, because they have been made the justification for the emotional fulfillment. But emotional factors will always win out as decision drivers, when they are made available and justifiable.

This strategy of recognizing the drivers of decisions that could be used, but are not now being used, is the single most powerful strategy available to any company for improving its revenue side. In our tests, this strategy was responsible for turning around products that had languished for more than a decade. It created growth in excess of 100 percent in many cases. (Although similar growth potential was available to many of our other test-bed companies, many did not want such growth and so they were able to limit the growth to a more manageable level.)

By focusing innovation not just on product development or quality improvement but also customer satisfaction and significance, dramatic growth potential was created—not just incremental growth that required constant maintenance and price management to sustain, but also exponential growth that sustained itself—in some cases with little or no further support from the marketer. In one case, a brand grew dramatically and then marketing support was purposely withdrawn to see what would happen. The brand maintained its new, higher level with minimal further support for another three years simply because the entire distribution network now believed so strongly in the product's power to create wealth for them that they supported it virtually on their own. Before that, the brand had required constant promotional support and continual nurturing of distributors to maintain any level of support from them.

> *Make customers feel smarter, bolder, braver, more influential, more knowledgeable, more admired, or more fulfilled, and customers will flock to your product.*

Figure 6 shows some of the powerful effects of improving influence through generating higher-level drivers of decisions. As marketers take more direct management control over driving expectations in order to create more influence for their brand, many benefits appear. Profit goes up. Competitive pressure goes down. Control over competitive decisions and competitive pressure increases. And margin for error goes up.

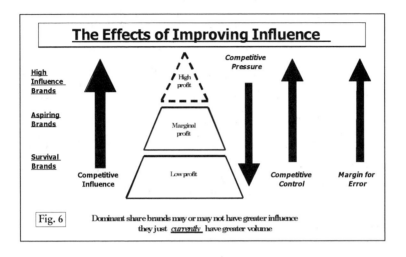

**The Effects of Improving Influence**

High Influence Brands

Aspiring Brands

Survival Brands

Competitive Pressure

High profit

Marginal profit

Low profit

Competitive Influence

Competitive Control

Margin for Error

Fig. 6    Dominant share brands may or may not have greater influence they just _currently_ have greater volume

This last factor is an often underestimated and undervalued benefit. Both Coca-Cola and Pepsi executives were shocked when they saw the immense margin for error that the Coke brand had created for itself over many years of being the Alpha in its category. In the 1980s, Pepsi had Coke on the ropes with a national campaign of blind taste tests that proved that loyal Coke drinkers actually didn't like Coke as much as they liked Pepsi. Coca-Cola executives, in desperation, decided to reformulate Coke to be more like Pepsi—a reaction that would have meant the end of Coke as the Alpha in the cola category and probably in the overall soft drink category as well. Unbelievably, customers rose up and demanded that the company bring back what came to be called Classic Coke. The company was saved from possibly the worst marketing blunder of all time by their customers. How many companies could expect that from their customers? It was all due to the immense margin for error created by being an Alpha.

By understanding the difference between current drivers of decisions and potential drivers that address higher-level needs, you can start driving more profitable customers to you, which drives even greater success and more control over the revenue side of your company. If you know that the current drivers of decisions include price, availability, and referral, but you change customer expectations to transform the drivers into satisfaction and significance factors such as a desire to buy the best there is (along with the knowledge to help customers discern this) or a feeling of being really appreciated by the company, suddenly the world you sell in has changed. Even if you don't have full distribution, people will seek you out. Even if your price is significantly higher than that of competitive products, people will find a way to pay for it. Even if your distributors did not previously recommend your product, they suddenly will be featuring it in their stores.

We've done this for so many products that I'm always surprised when I hear a corporate executive say he doesn't believe it can happen. We've seen products that had not shown any growth in more than a decade, despite heavy discounting and promotional effort, suddenly more than double sales without discounting or making changes in the product itself. Often, competitors just watch and wonder, not even knowing how to react, because what was just done was so far from the model

THE SECRET OF AN ALPHA

they embraced that they couldn't believe that what happened actually happened—at least not as the result of the causes that seemed to be at work.

If you focus innovation on providing the minimum product quality and performance required and the maximum satisfaction and significance fulfillment, you change everything. Suddenly, customers seek you out, competitors start to follow your lead, distributors support you because they believe in your ability to make them more successful, referral agents want the thanks they will receive from recommending you, and you start to experience a level of control over your future and that of others that you never imagined was possible. And when you make a mistake, you will be forgiven in ways that will finally make you believe that you are no longer alone in fighting for your company's success.

> *Focus innovation upon providing the* <u>*minimum*</u> *product quality and performance required, and* <u>*maximum*</u> *satisfaction and significance fulfillment. It changes everything.*

## SUMMARY

Alphas are created on the revenue side, not the cost side. To become an Alpha or simply to increase your competitive influence in your category, you need to re-define what customers should expect from a product in your category. You need to create a new vision of what is possible and become the provider of that. You can accomplish this by managing the emotional side of the decision process first and the rational side only as far as it needs to be managed in order to provide logical rationalization for purchase decisions.

Purchase decisions are driven primarily from the emotional side. These include both satisfaction and significance factors that make people feel more satisfied and more significant.

The way to become an Alpha (or just gain more of the benefits without actually being Alpha) is to manage *desired* drivers of decisions. That does not mean just knowing what the current drivers of decisions are—often they are not the ones that customers *wish* were at work. Understand what drivers of decisions could possibly be at work in your category in the future and that customers wish were at work now, and then manage your efforts to drive customers toward those. By doing so, you change customer expectations and take control of the category.

# 4

## ALPHA ASSETS—THE KEY TO MANAGING
## SELF-SUSTAINING GROWTH

Knowing the secret behind what creates Alpha influence is only the first step toward becoming successful at using it. In order to strategically drive and maintain self-sustaining success, there must be a set of things to track and manage—things that are critical to that success that must be monitored, protected, and modified as determined by changing market requirements. The things that any company aspiring to be or to remain as Alpha needs to manage are their Alpha Assets.

Alpha Assets are the causal factors that are driving your current success and, more important, that will drive future strategic growth beyond your current success. If you were to ask someone to list the most probable Alpha Assets companies should focus on, he would probably start with at least one successful product the company owns or sells. He might then talk about financial strength or relationship with distributors,

> *Alpha Assets are the real **causal** factors that drive current and future success.*

since it is all but impossible to create success without either deep pockets or a strong distribution network that will carry your product to end users. He might add that stellar management and innovation teams would be high on the priority list. He would probably then go on to cite efficient manufacturing operations that make it possible to be one of the lowest cost providers while maintaining one of the highest standards of quality in the industry.

In reality, none of these is a company's core Alpha Asset. None is the core causal factor that drives success. They may, at best, be supporting assets that sustain or prove the real Alpha Asset. The problem is that if these are the factors that are being managed, sustainable success will continue to be elusive.

In our research, we regularly measure over- or underperformance of products against customer expectations. Invariably we find that all but a few competitors in a category are performing at or above expectations in quality, functional performance, and price. There is little meaningful differentiation going on as a result of these factors, which most companies believe are critical to success. Where most, if not all, competitors typically underperform is in customer expectations for satisfaction and significance factors.

Interestingly, Alphas always perform well in these two sets of emotional factors. Some have been Alphas for so long that they and their customers may not even recognize just how strong the brand or product is in addressing self-satisfaction and significance. The revelation is when customers can't get the product, and the way they react to that fact.

We almost always ask research participants how they would react if the product or brand they usually buy was not available at the place they usually shop. Corporate managers have laughed at the idea that anyone might be willing to drive somewhere else to get their favorite brand, yet a large percentage of customers for Alphas and strong aspiring brands would drive somewhere else to buy their brand. The only times this failed to prove out was when participants didn't believe they would have to wait more than a few days or when they didn't know of any other place they could possibly get that product within a reasonable distance, and they could just go back at a later date and get it. The percentage of customers who would travel to buy a non-Alpha product somewhere else (or even wait to buy it rather than a competitive product) decreases as

> *Loyalty is really tested by how customers react when they can't get your product.*

you move from aspiring brands to survival brands. Typically, among survival brands there is so little loyalty that customers say they would just buy something else rather than wait or search it out.

Understanding what your real Alpha Assets are is critical to managing and maintaining them. Alpha Assets are the experiences someone has with a company, product, or brand that lead to high-level self-satisfaction and personal significance. They are not the things that we have traditionally been taught to think of as drivers of revenue-side success.

You might sell a product that is considered one of the best in the category (of high quality and high "value"). That product may even command a high price and have made you the top share marketer in that category. But as soon as another product comes along that is "better," what happens to your share and your company's future growth potential? Only the experience that defines what the product means to its user can sustain a product beyond actual features and benefits.

Victoria's Secret sells clothing that makes a woman feel sexier and more attractive. Even if the quality were higher than it is, someone could easily make better-quality clothing that looks similar or even more attractive than theirs. That improvement by a competitor would not quickly have the effect of significantly harming either Victoria's Secret's market share or their future profitability, because their customers aren't buying a product; they are buying an experience of self-satisfaction and significance.

Here's a more commercial example. There was a time when Celotex was the most visibly used brand in new home construction for exterior sheathing (the insulating board that goes on the outside of a house before siding is attached). Many competitors tried desperately to wedge their way into that lucrative market, but they continually ran into a significant barrier to entry: Older workers (and younger ones who respected the older workers with whom they worked) didn't want to see brands changed. The reason behind this turned out to have nothing to do with quality of product or price or ease of installation or anything other than the fact that "real construction guys use Celotex." This belief was not held among the actual decision makers for purchasing, but, rather, among the people who had to work with the product and who obviously had a great deal of influence on what would be applied to a house they were building. Celotex really did little to maintain that perception over the years, so eventually, as the older workers retired and younger ones came on without loyalty to the brand, Celotex eventually lost the hold it had, and it is now just one of many lesser brands being used. However, while the belief existed that you were a "real construction guy" if you used that product, there was a very high barrier to entry for a new brand.

Obviously, not all companies have Alpha Assets, because not all companies enter the marketplace with the desire to drive expectations or to create a dominant place for themselves. Most survival and scavenger brands only have the purpose of making money from what is left behind after all the stronger brands have taken their share. I got to know the owner of a business who had made a lot of money over the years simply by building scavenger brands and then selling the company. All the companies had one purpose: Take advantage of the work someone else had done in creating a market opportunity and then underprice them significantly with a look-alike product that would capture just enough sales to make a saleable business. His companies were never major players, and they didn't really frighten the major players or make much of a dent in their market share. He made himself wealthy on the small percentage of fringe customers who wanted to believe they could get by with something that simply looked like the higher-quality product and pocket the price difference.

> *Understanding the difference between "normal" assets and Alpha assets is extremely important to building a company beyond the scavenger level.*

He could have chosen to develop Alpha Assets if he had really wanted to grow dramatically and had been able to maintain that new level of success for a long period of time. But his strategy was simply to make a business thrive just enough and then sell it before the tough part of keeping the business alive from a scavenger position really started.

Understanding the difference between normal demand-creation assets and Alpha Assets is extremely important in building a company beyond the scavenger level. Every aspiring brand has some of these assets; that's why they have been able to create enough strength to rise above the scavenger or survival level to become at least a noticeable player in their respective category. The real battle of supremacy is at the highest level: the Core Alpha Asset. Sustaining that core asset are all of the Supporting Alpha Assets that the company has.

## THE CORE ALPHA ASSET

Every company that has been able to create a loyal following for reasons other than price or convenient availability has a Core Alpha Asset. It may not be one that makes it strong enough to become the Alpha of the category, but it has something that makes it capable of creating loyalty among at least a niche segment of customers.

When a company, product, or brand is consistent enough in the way it offers products or services to the market, customers begin to expect a specific range of experience from it. The more clearly differentiated that experience is from the way competitors offer their products or services, the easier it is for customers to become loyal to it. The more that experience comes close to defining what it means to buy a product in that category in terms of both minimal functionality and high levels of self-satisfaction and significance, the closer that company moves toward becoming the Alpha of the category.

> *Before successful branding can even be considered, the core Alpha Asset has to be created and defined.*

This is the real battle for supremacy on the revenue side. Can you create a strong enough Core Alpha Asset for your product, brand, or company to drive category-wide expectations so that more and more competitors start to follow your lead, giving you the control?

Let me stop for a moment and say that we are not talking about branding here. This is the basic element that makes successful branding possible for a company or product. Before successful branding can even be considered, the Core Alpha Asset has to be created and defined. Many brands go through their entire existence without there ever being a Core Alpha Asset behind it. That's why marketing communications can never create or sustain a company. They can only inform potential customers, distributors, and referral agents about what has already been created.

Harley-Davidson certainly provides the Alpha-style experience to its customers. Almost anyone riding a Harley does so with the expectation of minimum functionality (no one expects a Harley to be the most comfortable or the most technologically advanced bike on the road), but, more important, he expects that he will be admired, respected, and perhaps a little feared by friends, acquaintances, and people who happen to see him pass by. Even other motorcyclists riding other makes of bikes would typically be expected to show them respect.

BMW motorcycle purchasers expect something very different. Although these are actually part of another class of bikes (touring versus cruisers), they are purchased by people who want to experience a much better ride quality on long treks, along with the pride that goes with riding one of the most technologically advanced, beautifully styled, best-engineered, and most expensive touring motorcycles in the world.

> *The battle of Core Alpha Assets in the marketplace is based upon which experience provides more and higher satisfaction and significance.*

Both Harley-Davidson and BMW motorcycles have Core Alpha Assets that drive expectations for self-satisfaction and personal significance. No other manufacturer of cruiser or touring motorcycles seems to have a Core Alpha Asset, because everyone else seems to be following the lead of these two motorcycle manufacturers in these categories.

Why does Harley-Davidson's Core Alpha Asset win over

BMW's with the largest percentage of the population? Its strength has actually made cruisers the dominant category for motorcycles. More cruisers are sold each year than any other category of motorcycle. Harley-Davidson has accomplished this simply because it addresses more personal significance factors than any other motorcycle. BMW addresses more self-satisfaction factors, but significance overrides satisfaction. Riding a Harley is all about significance: A new Harley owner immediately feels stronger, more formidable, more attractive, more respected, and a whole lot of other things that mean a high level of personal significance. Riding a BMW is all about being smart and self-satisfied—a BMW owner knows he has a better product than almost anything else out there, with features that most people never dreamed might be available on a motorcycle (such as a power-tilting windshield), but few other people know about it. He rides down the road laughing to himself about the poor owners of other motorcycles who are missing out on the great experience he is having. He feels self-satisfied (significant in his own eyes), while the Harley owner feels significant *and* self-satisfied because he believes everyone else thinks better of him for owning one.

This battle of Core Alpha Assets is all based on which experience provides more and higher levels of satisfaction and significance. As we saw earlier, satisfaction and significance seem to work side by side in the decision process, but when some level of self-satisfaction is already there, significance will be the deciding factor.

Managing this Core Alpha experience and keeping it fresh and relevant is the key. Any company—but especially the Alpha company—that allows this Core Alpha Asset to be diminished risks losing its status, influence, and control over the category.

When Armstrong World Industries was the Alpha of their category, they completely dominated decisions about resilient flooring, especially for residential applications although they were also the top-selling commercial brand. At their peak, 80 percent of the U.S. population would name Armstrong first when asked to name a flooring brand. Every other competitor followed their lead, and few had any real brand loyalty of their own. Almost all competitors simply offered lower-priced alternatives to what was clearly considered by consumers, distributors, referral agents, and competitors, to be the top choice in resilient flooring. Armstrong had enough leverage with distributors that they could demand that their distributors sell no competitive line of product. They had enough leverage with retailers that it was critical for a retailer to carry Armstrong product in order to compete in the flooring business.

Today, few consumers even recognize the brand. Although it is still sold by many retailers in the business, it is certainly not the featured or lead brand.

What happened? Armstrong lost sight of the need to maintain their Core Alpha Asset.

So what was this Core Alpha Asset that they lost? It wasn't a problem with their product. Armstrong's product was certainly of high quality and its performance was functionally above average for the category. The company itself was devoted to quality and performance excellence—it won the Malcolm Baldrige award as it was in the process of losing its Alpha status and becoming just another brand. The Core Alpha Asset that Armstrong forgot was the experience of believing you could make your home beautiful enough to be a *Better Homes & Gardens* or *Southern Living* magazine centerfold. From 1918 until they gave up their prime advertising positions in the top shelter magazines in the 1980s, Armstrong led the industry by convincing women that they could be interior designers and make all their friends envy them for having such a beautiful home.

Armstrong's print ads were elaborate room sets that included cutting-edge ideas for how to decorate and live elegantly. Women studied those ads for hours to get ideas and to understand how the look and feel of the room had been achieved. At its peak, Armstrong received so many requests from home owners for information about items and decorating ideas in the ads that the company actually decided to start a magazine and catalog of decorating items to capitalize on this unmet need.

In the 1980s, an Armstrong CEO who believed that the

real core asset of the company was its superior product decided to stop supporting this strategic asset. The result was that Armstrong slipped from its top position within a short period of time.

Sears forgot about its Core Alpha Asset in the 1970s after being the Alpha in its category for about two decades. What was it that set Sears apart and made it the Alpha? Was it the company's top-rated Kenmore appliances? Its Craftsman hand tools, which were the first choice of home mechanics and many professionals? Its Easy Living paint that was the best-selling paint in the country? How about its presence in almost every town in America with either a full retail store or a smaller catalog sales office? None of these. Actually, its Core Alpha Asset changed over the years, just getting better and better. At the start this Core Alpha Asset was the significance customers felt by being granted credit when few other stores would (this was before credit cards came along) and being able to buy high-quality products that would otherwise have been beyond their means. Eventually, the Core Alpha Asset evolved into the experience of shopping at the American icon, where customers could buy top-quality products that were not just off the shelf from some supplier but instead were custom-designed to give middle-class Americans better quality for money, along with the confidence that they were covered by a money-back guarantee—another experience that enhanced the sense of personal significance and self-satisfaction.

What caused Sears to blow their Alpha position was not their relentless pursuit of more profit despite driving prices beyond their customers' reach. Nor was it even forgetting that their opening-price-point products were proof of the value Sears offered everyone, regardless of income level; they made their advertised opening-price-point items harder and harder to buy. The real clincher was when they made themselves "Brand Central," filling the stores with national brands that competed with their own. They were no longer different or better or anything other than just another department store.

Along the way, as Sears slowly forgot what they represented and why customers shopped there, they gave upstart Kmart room to enter the market. If Sears had not neglected their critical opening-price-point strategy that made them appear to be an option for every American home (despite the fact that they sold relatively few of those items and, frankly, didn't want to sell them), Kmart would not have had a business opportunity. Unfortunately, Kmart followed Sears' strategic approach far too closely—right down to their continual upscaling and disregard for their core customer base and Core Alpha Asset. That error left the opening for Wal-Mart to enter the mainstream, after having been relegated primarily to smaller tertiary markets.

Coca-Cola almost lost its Alpha status when it jettisoned its classic formula, not realizing that flavor was the key to its Core Alpha Asset: memories of hot summer days and being refreshed with an ice-cold Coke (that's what many customers said when they begged Coca-Cola to bring back the "real" Coke after they dropped it in favor of New Coke). Luckily, Coca-Cola was able to backtrack and recover before they lost everything they had gained over almost 100 years as a company.

These Core Alpha Assets all sound silly when put through the filter of rational thinking and belief that product, price, promotion, and availability are the core assets that must be managed. But we saw over and over again that none of those things have a fraction of the impact and influence of core experiences that drive self-satisfaction and personal significance among customers.

We experimented with many companies to create such Core Alpha Assets. It's almost embarrassing how simple the solution sounds in the face of the dramatic results that were generated. But anyone who has ever labored to discover a solution that really works knows that the simpler the solution sounds, the harder it generally is to discover and implement.

As already mentioned in passing, we took a regional ice cream brand of a national marketer that had tested out as the worst-tasting ice cream in the market and helped the company make it number one in just a few months while cutting discounting and without changing the product formulation until after growth occurred. We achieved this simply by creating a new expectation that we had discovered was core to the ice cream experience and unmet in the marketplace: homemade taste. Again, this might sound silly, but we discovered that customers wanted so badly to reclaim the memory of sitting on the back porch with grandma and grandpa making ice cream that they overcame the actual taste of this product and made it their favorite. The company's retailers were so convinced that this promised experience would draw customers to whatever store carried the product that they gave the marketer shelf space for added product without slotting fees, reduced the promotional allowances that were normally required of their suppliers, cut down on the amount of discounting required, offered them free ad space in their promotional flyers, and gave them a high-visibility shelf position. The result was a dramatic increase in sales and profit for the product, significant traffic for retailers that carried this product, and new customer loyalty that provided the brand with enough leverage that retailers. wanted to ride its coattails into the next selling season.

Filtered through an assumption that product, price, promotion, availability, or any of the other rational elements of marketing are the drivers of success, this sounds absurd. We hit only the self-satisfaction factor with this particular strategy, yet no one else in the regular premium ice cream category had done even that. But it is exactly that simplicity that makes it so hard for most companies to approach the process of becoming an Alpha. They are focused on all the wrong things. And then along comes a company out of nowhere that mysteriously captures the imagination and loyalty of customers with a strong Core Alpha Asset that addresses higher levels of self-satisfaction and significance than anyone else has achieved, and it becomes the decision leader in the category.

Ben & Jerry's did it. They were a small company in the middle of nowhere with a couple of ex-hippies making quirky ice cream flavors, yet they captured both the self-satisfaction and significance factors that customers were seeking and were not receiving from other major brands in the category.

Harley-Davidson did it. Although they had been considered a top brand in the 1950s (as one of their 1950s advertisements stated, "The only thing that can catch a Harley is another Harley"), but their product quality was so far below minimum functionality that they were all but out of business when employees bought the company from AMF in the early 1980s. While Japanese bikes had overrun U.S. markets and changed expectations for what was considered a "good" motorcycle, Harley-Davidson suddenly started to grow significantly by increasing quality to at least the functional minimums (still nowhere near the quality, rear-wheel power, and technology of Japanese bikes) and helping a new generation of motorcyclists discover the hidden rebel within them. They captured the unmet needs for self-satisfaction and personal significance that men of all ages were looking for and enabled anyone who was willing to spend the outrageous premium price for a Harley to attain that.

Victoria's Secret did it. Frederick's of Hollywood had been around for years selling sexy women's clothes through small-format ads in magazines. They still exist, but not many people know that fact because Victoria's Secret made being sexy mainstream, not something to be hidden in the back of magazines. They addressed the needs for higher-level self-satisfaction and personal significance by making it acceptable to buy sexy women's clothing, even something a woman (or boyfriend) would be proud to let others know.

Sears did it. Coming out of World War II, Montgomery Ward was the king of general merchandise retailing. Sears was still primarily a "farmer's" store, selling a huge percentage of their product through small stores, a catalog, and catalog sales offices in small towns all over America. The real reason they became the top retailer in the world by the end of the 1950s was that they addressed the need for personal significance of Americans who were anxious to improve their lifestyle, but who needed credit to be able to obtain the good life they so desperately desired.

The trouble is that the Core Alpha Asset must be supported and maintained, or it will disappear. That requires, first, recognizing it as the asset that must be protected above all else, and, second, keeping it fresh and alive in the minds of customers. It's not that hard to do, as long as you continue to recognize the need, but backing up and trying to retake ground that was given away is costly and not always possible.

Sears will probably never become a lead retailer again. Neither will Kmart. Coca-Cola has never quite recovered from helping to make Pepsi the solid alternative to Coke. And Celotex will probably never regain the hold it had on the home building industry. It's also doubtful that Armstrong could ever again regain its position as the Alpha of flooring. Once a company has sacrificed its Core Alpha Asset and become either an aspiring brand or a survival/scavenger brand, it is extremely hard to regain what it lost. It's not impossible in theory, but it would be extremely difficult. Doing so would require a complete reinvention of the company, negating all the mistakes it made and making the marketplace forget what it used to represent.

That happened for U.S. Savings Bonds. The product had been a common and quite popular method of saving as World War II ended. Almost every child in the 1950s and early '60s had U.S. Savings Bonds stamps, which they saved until they had enough to redeem for a $25 Savings Bond. Payroll savings plans at most places of employment were also very popular ways to put money aside out of each paycheck to buy U.S. Savings Bonds. It was like a mandatory plan to make sure you had something saved at the end of each month. Once the stock market started to take off in the 1980s, all that changed. What had once been a smart way to save had become a product for "losers" who weren't smart enough or didn't earn enough to invest in the stock market. By the early

1990s, financial writers were calling U.S. Savings Bonds "the worst financial product in the U.S." In fact, an entire industry sprang up to bash Savings Bonds and teach people how to get rid of them in favor of "smarter" products. Compounding that was the fact that the primary distribution channel for the bonds (banks) had no incentive to sell them. Most bank tellers were trained to instantly convert anyone who asked about a U.S. Savings Bond into a certificate of deposit customer. Sales were quickly declining at a double-digit rate despite the fact that $55 billion in Savings Bonds were held by Americans.

The U.S. Department of the Treasury turned that completely around by creating a way for anyone fearful of the stock market to feel both smart and significant—that included both the low end of the savings market and the high end of investors. The research we did showed that there was a strong fear of both the volatility in the stock market and the effects of inflation on savings and investments (even during periods of low inflation).

Out of that was created the I Bond, an inflation-adjusted product that provides a guaranteed return above the rate of inflation, unlike any other savings or investment products available. Two new distribution channels were also created to overcome the problem of having to sell through competitors: online investing, which alone accounted for more than $2 million per week in sales after less than six months, and EasySaver, which was essentially a payroll savings plan for individuals who did not have access to such a plan at work. This allows people to sign up for automatic purchases of Savings Bonds without having to go to their bank or computer.

Suddenly, financial writers were calling this a smart savings product that was right for the time. People who hated to admit that they wanted to buy something safe had a way to accomplish that, and savvy investors had a smart, low-cost method of protecting their gains against inflation. The product started growing so strongly that Congress did not even see the need to maintain the public service advertising funding that had been used to promote sales of the product.

Today, U.S. Savings Bonds are not on the tip of everyone's tongue. Nor are they the first vehicle most Americans would choose for saving, but by focusing on addressing unmet needs for self-satisfaction and personal significance rather than just raising rates or making them more widely available, the Treasury was able to dramatically turn around a product that seemed doomed to a slow death.

Cadillac is trying desperately to regain some of the lost influence it once had. Up until the 1970s, Cadillac was considered one of the premier automobiles in the world. Cadillac was the car that most men aspired to own (not only in America, but also in many other parts of the world), and women wanted to be seen riding in one. The company went on autopilot in the late 1960s and forgot to keep that experience fresh, so they lost it to a myriad of other brands, eventually becoming less than an afterthought to anyone under the age of 40. They realized their mistake recently and came back strong by applying the Cadillac experience to younger drivers. They redesigned the product to be less of a "big boat" and made it more performance-oriented, even entering racing again. They did not make the mistake of simply trying to relabel a tired old product, as Oldsmobile did. (Recall the pathetic slogan, "This is not your father's Oldsmobile," which only made everyone notice that it actually was just that.) Instead, they proved the product's desirability with fast, sexy-looking cars (at least to many people's taste) that promised the experience of being admired and liked by others. Their advertising messages, meant to change perceptions of the product, often showed middle-aged friends having fun in obviously high-brow situations. Although it took a while to have an effect, this approach eventually started to work, drawing in more than just seniors who remembered the dreams of the 1950s.

The significance factor remains a critical part of the Cadillac Core Alpha Asset. It simply has not yet been translated effectively enough to overtake the many other brands that established themselves more firmly while Cadillac slept. Brands like Lexus, Infinity, Mercedes-Benz, and BMW all have far stronger significance factors in their Core Alpha Assets.

## SUPPORTING ALPHA ASSETS

Every company that has a Core Alpha Asset also has critical Supporting Alpha Assets. These are the things that help sustain and continually *prove* the Core Alpha Asset to customers, distributors, referral agents, and competitors. Without them, the Core Alpha Asset is just an empty claim that soon disappears in the reality of actual experience.

Supporting Alpha Assets could include almost anything— any contact (direct or indirect) with current or potential customers, the way the product is distributed, where the product is made, and even the product's color. There are actually 19 sets of Supporting Alpha Assets that can be grouped into four general categories: Needs Satisfaction, Communications Effectiveness, Differentiation, and Loyalty Generation. Each of these 19 sets of potential Supporting Alpha Assets can be defined, measured, and tracked over time for changes through research, and each helps indicate how influential a company is now and what can potentially be improved to better support its Core Alpha Asset.

# THE 19 SETS OF SUPPORTING ALPHA ASSETS

Needs Satisfaction—
- Product performance
- Profitability available to users and distributors
- Availability
- Price
- Quality
- People involved in contact with customers and distributors
- Purpose for which the product is used
- Packaging

Communications Effectiveness—any purposeful marketing communications
- Seen or heard communications
- Persuasiveness of communications (any and all used)
- Effectiveness of packaging
- Personality of the product, brand, or company

Differentiation—
- How different it is
- What makes it different (is it a rational or an emotional factor and how high is the level of emotional satisfaction/significance)
- The perceptual arena the brand, product, or company "owns"

Loyalty Generation—
- How well-known it is
- How resistant customers are to competitive pressure
- Problems encountered and how effectively they are solved
- Anticipated future purchasing

For each Alpha, the critical Supporting Alpha Assets may be quite different. For instance, quality is critical to proving the Core Alpha Asset of Mercedes-Benz. It is not critical to the core Alpha Asset of Harley-Davidson. For Victoria's Secret, the models are a critical Supporting Alpha Asset. For Wal-Mart, similar models would only confuse or offend their customers. Each Alpha has its own set of critical Supporting Alpha Assets that it must recognize, maintain, and protect at almost any cost.

Harley-Davidson is one of the best-known Alphas in the world. Almost anyone could list the Core Alpha Asset it holds: an "I can take on the world" confidence and attitude. Most people who buy a Harley motorcycle want others to think of them that way, and they buy a Harley because it helps them communicate that message to anyone who sees them on that bike. I've never met anyone who bought one because they considered it the most technologically advanced machine available. I've never met anyone who bought one because it was the best buy on the market (although the effect of its Alpha status has been that resale value is stronger than for most other motorcycles). I've never met anyone who bought one because it is the most comfortable bike to ride. No matter what they say initially about their reason for buying, they eventually admit that they bought a Harley because they wanted others to respect them. We're not talking about insecurity any more than buying a shirt or purse with a logo on it represents insecurity. It's a basic human need for ego satisfaction and communication of who we believe we are or want to become.

Backing up that Core Alpha Asset are many Supporting Alpha Assets. It's not just the company's advertising; it's every Harley rider who wears black leather. It's every story told about Harley riders being treated with respect. It's the deep rumble of the Harley exhaust system that can be heard two miles away. It's seeing a young guy run across his yard to give a thumbs-up to a passing Harley rider. The more people hear about the experience of driving a Harley, the more people they know who have ridden to Sturgis for the annual gathering, the more times they hear a large group of Harleys rumbling down the street together and rattling windows with their roar, the more Supporting Alpha Assets are being created for the brand that build loyalty among customers and envy or aspiration among noncustomers. That's why Harley-Davidson took steps to patent the characteristic sound of its exhaust system. Allow another brand to copy that, and the uniqueness of the Harley experience would be diminished.

Harley's Supporting Alpha Assets also include the ability to customize their bikes and the regular events throughout the year that allow fellow riders to show off their customizations. When I still rode one, I never missed the annual open house. You couldn't pay for a better show—hundreds of bikes roaring along the highways and pulling in to park side by side in the field next to the plant, people in crazy outfits, engine revving contests. Anyone who witnessed this event, even if they didn't join in, was either disgusted by it or wanted to buy a Harley and participate.

Ben & Jerry's Supporting Alpha Assets are the crazy flavors and quirky names they come up with for them. The high price of their products is another Supporting Alpha Asset—they would lose much of their value if they were priced at the level of all those "lesser" brands. The fact that the founders were a couple of ex-hippies helped, but it wasn't critical to their success—it merely added more "flavor" to their quirkiness.

As already outlined, Armstrong's Supporting Alpha Assets included their advertising in the same prime position each month in all the most important shelter magazines that showed new decorating ideas far beyond the floors, carpeting, and ceilings that they were trying to sell. They also had a strong and loyal distribution network that sold no competitive products and was devoted to the brand, because it was making them wealthy.

Victoria's Secret's Supporting Alpha Assets include the models they use in their advertising and merchandising. Their prime locations in high-profile shopping malls rather than hiding in strip malls on the periphery of the primary mall are also a critical Supporting Alpha Asset because the company is bold in flaunting their sexuality message.

Coca-Cola did not recognize that its flavor was a key Supporing Alpha Asset—no matter how much people said they preferred the taste of Pepsi. If it weren't for their ultraloyal customer base, the company's core Alpha Asset would have disappeared, because New Coke didn't remind anyone of hot summer days during childhood when you'd drink an ice-cold Coke that burned your throat but tasted so good.

Could any of those Alphas survive for long without their Supporting Alpha Assets? Probably not. If Victoria's Secret started using models who looked like real people, they certainly would not maintain their influence. If Harley-Davidson made their bikes so that they ran perfectly smooth and quiet, they would quickly fail because that doesn't reflect their Core Alpha Asset.

Some Alphas, like Wal-Mart, have a more fragile hold on their position, since their Supporting Alpha Assets are more vulnerable than those held by many other Alphas. Price is clearly a Supporting Alpha Asset for Wal-Mart, although their core Alpha Asset transcends price alone. This has been the weakness of every retail Alpha that focused on price—sooner or later, someone comes along and beats them on price and one or more of their other critical Supporting Alpha Assets. The result is always the slow demise of the company.

Losing or forgetting to protect critical Supporting Alpha Assets is the top cause of past Alphas losing their influential position and slipping into mediocrity. It doesn't always happen quickly, which just adds to the confusion for market analysts—but it always happens.

## HARVESTING—THE TERRIBLE TOOL OF DESTRUCTION FOR ALPHAS

Probably the most devastating way Alphas have been killed over the past few decades has been through what I call "harvesting." Harvesting is the practice by top managers of killing Supporting Alpha Assets, taking the "savings," and putting it toward the bottom line to gain short-term profit. The idea is either to boost stock prices or to generate a large bonus for top management at the expense of the company itself. These misguided managers are simply harvesting the value of the Core Alpha Asset at a real cost to the company of its very future.

The reason the company gains anything from this practice is that the Core Alpha Asset maintains its value for some time even after the Supporting Alpha Assets have been killed. The company's demise doesn't come immediately. It takes time for people either to realize that the Alpha is no longer satisfying their needs or to become so distracted by other competing brands and products that they lose their past loyalty or aspirations to own it.

The way this works is deceptively simple, and stock analysts don't seem to be all that aware of the effects this practice will generate because they don't seem at all concerned about its prevalent use in boosting short-term stock prices while harming long-term profits. That's probably why the practice is so heavily used among major corporations today. Most of this is driven by pressure from the stock market—or, more accurately, from large-block investors, who demand short-term gains even at the cost of the future of the company. After all, they don't care what happens to the company *after* they sell the stock; they are advocates of the company only as long as they want to see prices go up. Once the prices are high enough, they sell and then go elsewhere to demand higher short-term profit performance from another company.

Here's how harvesting works:

An inventory is made of anything that might be eliminated to cut short-term costs and allow a profit-and-loss statement to show higher bottom-line profit performance. Cuts can include advertising, staff, facilities, depreciation reserves, or just about anything else. Many of those items may be critical Supporting Alpha Assets that sustain the Core Alpha Asset, but that is often obscured by the *correct* belief that the company, product, or brand can survive for some time without that support but the

> *Harvesting the value of its Core Alpha Asset costs the company its very future.*

*flawed* belief that it would be easy to restore those supporting assets later and reclaim the past influence they generated. Unfortunately, although a company, product, or brand can survive for a while without the supporting assets that kept it at its high level of influence, once lost, simply restoring the supporting assets seldom restores the value that was once there. It takes far longer and more investment to create an Alpha than it does to kill one.

In terms of company value, the loss of these assets immediately diminishes the long-term value of the company even though the short-term value might appear to be greater due to higher bottom-line profitability. It is like selling off one wheel from your car in order to pay for gas. The loss of the supporting assets that drive the value-generating power of a company makes it much harder and more expensive to ever recoup what was lost as a result of that short-term gain.

The thing that makes harvesting at all attractive is the fact that it takes a long time for the real damage to be recognized. The residual benefits of having once created Alpha Assets are strong enough that the managers who kill them are often gone by the time the full impact of the consequences is felt.

I watched one smaller Alpha take three years to drop back to its previous low starting point after it took away the Supporting Alpha Assets that would have sustained that value. It took them only one year to become the Alpha, but it took three years to lose the entire benefit of it. They thought they were pretty smart about it. However, they overlooked that they had lost the decades of benefit they could have had from increased profitability—they had more than doubled their profit margins and had dramatically grown their market share. Those were sacrificed for a short-term gain that then had to be re-created in other, more expensive ways in future years.

Frankly, I believe it will not be until stock analysts and stockholders recognize this truth and begin to analyze how short-term profits are really being driven in a company that values will become more aligned with the reality of the future growth potential of a company. This devastating and self-destructive short-term profit generation practice of harvesting will only continue to undermine the strength of American businesses unless the real causes of the demise of past Alphas is recognized and clearly understood.

## SUMMARY

By recognizing your current and potential Alpha Assets, the actual causal factors that are driving your success and the ones that will drive even greater long-term self-sustaining growth, you can strategically manage the revenue side of your business. Alpha Assets are more than just attributes that can be measured easily. They are also the deep, core factors customers might reveal that show why they are buying your product over someone else's. The core drivers of decisions are the experiences customers have with your product, company, or brand.

Alpha Assets are heavily skewed toward self-satisfaction

and significance to the point that they drive expectations for the category. Even when product performance and quality seem to be key differentiators, the real core drivers behind that strength are the satisfaction and personal significance that the customer receives from that performance or quality. Forget that, and you risk falling back down the ladder to become a survival brand.

Learn what your real Alpha Assets are (not the ones you imagine them to be) and manage them relentlessly. Just as you would manage any other investment assets, your Alpha Assets must be given higher priority over almost any other consideration. They are the lifeblood of your company's future success. Understand your Core Alpha Asset and make it the thing that is never compromised. Understand what your Supporting Alpha Assets are and make sure that if you change any of them, you have not undermined the Core Alpha Asset.

Avoid the temptation to harvest the value from brands and products that have been built to influential levels in the past. The gains generated can never offset the long-term destruction to the brand, product, and company.

# 5

## RULES FOR STRATEGIC APPLICATION
## OF ALPHA LEARNING

Recognizing an Alpha is one thing. Using the learning about what creates an Alpha is quite another, especially if you don't believe you can become the overall Alpha of your category. Possibly the most amazing thing about what we learned in the Alpha Factor Project was that almost any company can benefit from understanding the underlying principles of becoming an Alpha. Not all companies that use this learning will become Alphas, but they all have the potential to geometrically increase their revenue stream and profitability.

Consistently, we discovered that there is a set of rules and foundational factors that must be followed to be successful in using this learning. Where these rules were not followed, there was either no success or the success was short-lived. This chapter lists the critical rules and the foundational factors that consistently led to success using Alpha learning.

## FOUNDATIONAL FACTORS

The biggest obstacle to success, we discovered, was self-limitation. Either the company was determined to follow a wrongheaded model that continually pushed it back into a *following* position, or it just did not believe it could or should be as successful as possible. I can't even count the number of times we heard CEOs say, "Thanks, but we'll take it from here," only to fall right back into the strategic model that had kept them from success in the first place. Where an organization wanted to hold on to old-model approaches, they either completely undermined the success that was created, taking their revenue generation back to pre-Alpha model days, or they significantly limited the success they realized. The organizations that saw the greatest sustainable success were those that embraced the new way of thinking in the Alpha model and made it fundamental to their day-to-day decision making and measurements of performance.

Next was the problem of aligning all revenue generation processes, measurements, incentives, and management. This was always a difficult foundational hurdle facing the organizations with which we applied Alpha learning. The commitment of top executives to managing by this model was always the key factor in the longevity of the success this model created in our test organizations. The sustainability of success was always tied to how long managers tracked results based on the Alpha model, measuring performance in self-satisfaction and personal significance as the ultimate driver of success and all other factors only as support to that. The less change that was made to innovation and other revenue-side processes, measurements, incentives, and management focus, the shorter the success generated by following Alpha learning. Those who took the revenue gains generated as just one more promotional effort rather than part of a major change in how the organization was run never saw long-term success.

We also learned that the greatest success came to organizations where top managers took credit for that success and made the maintenance of that success their own. Contrary to the theories that top managers should avoid taking credit for organizational success, we discovered that this was critical to sustainable success. These managers were the most likely to go back to the Alpha model in times of challenge rather than immediately falling back on the old model of thinking. They were also the most likely to train others to understand the new model and make it part of the organizational culture. Much as Jack Welch did by making Six Sigma the core tool used throughout the GE organization, the Alpha model must become the revenue-side model for continuing management of performance improvement.

---

## Rule #1: Functionally satisfy at least the minimum; emotionally satisfy the maximum.

---

If you haven't got it yet, satisfy at least the minimum in terms of functional expectations (and those change over time). Once you've accomplished that, satisfy emotional needs, especially these for self-satisfaction and personal significance. Having the best product won't create an Alpha, even for the first company to market it. The first to market often has a significant advantage for the initial few months, if it is smart about marketing and has been lucky enough to have found the best solution to whatever functional need it is addressing. But the emotional needs satisfaction must follow quickly for there to be any hope of becoming an expectation setter—the first step in becoming an Alpha.

The company that first introduced the after-shower spray that keeps your shower stall clean never made that move from functional to emotional needs. It performed better than any competitor that I tried in the first few years of its existence, but we moved on because there was no emotional satisfaction being addressed. My wife quickly found alternatives that did a satisfactory job at a lower price. She then tried several other brands to see whether anything worked better. She finally settled on a brand that cost more than the original ever did and worked only about as well as the original. The only emotional satisfaction we get out of this new product is that it is a major national brand, but that's far too weak a benefit to overcome a strong competitive attack. Any marketer who comes along and fulfills more of the needs for self-satisfaction and personal significance with this type of product will be able to make tremendous gains at the cost of the many competitors that have invested in the category. It is telling that I can no longer even recall the name of that original company.

If functional needs satisfaction were the true differentiator of top brands and survival brands, Coke would not be an Alpha—Pepsi clearly proved that it was preferred in blind taste tests. Neither would McDonald's—there are many alternatives that provide better food at comparable prices. Nor would Harley-Davidson—almost any other motorcycle in the world is engineered better than a Harley.

To work toward becoming an Alpha, you must meet at least minimum functional needs *and* also provide higher levels of satisfaction and significance. Minimum functional requirements may change over time depending on expectations being set by the competitive environment, so you must keep track of functional expectations. You have to go further than simply offering a product that performs well, however; you must make customers feel smart, appreciated, more attractive (or more respected), and/or more "fulfilled." Alphas always seem to meet more higher-level needs than their competitors. Where that higher-level needs satisfaction is not deep and strong, such as with Wal-Mart, its Alpha status is tenuous. No matter how strong Wal-Mart seems right now, it will eventually be replaced by another low-price retailer, just as Sears was by Kmart. The only way Wal-Mart can avoid that is to build deeper Supporting Alpha Assets that satisfy more and higher-level emotional needs. As long as the Alpha in a category focuses on maintaining that differentiation by addressing the highest level of emotional needs satisfaction in the category, it will remain an Alpha. As soon as it loses that focus and becomes caught up in competing to meet lower-level needs, it begins to lose its Alpha status.

---

## Rule #2: Don't compete on price.

---

Yes, you will be forced to use price discounting just to maintain your retailer or distributor relationships at times. But Alphas don't gain or maintain their Alpha status based on price alone. In fact, they compete less on price than their competitors. Price-focused marketing is the realm of survival brands that try to scavenge the pieces left by more influential brands and products. Any company setting price as its differentiation point is lost before it starts. Sooner or later, someone else will become the low-price provider and take over that point of differentiation.

As we have already noted, even though Wal-Mart is typically seen as the low-price retailer, their Alpha status is not based on that. In fact, they are not the true low-price provider in most product categories. They just use that perception to support their true Alpha Assets of making people feel smart for not spending more, for having to go to only one place to get most of what they need, and for getting great-quality products that can be returned easily if they are not satisfied with them. Kmart used to have a similar perception among the buying public, but they lost it once they made the return process difficult, tried to push their margins too high, and then started cutting inventories in their stores.

Don't get confused about the importance of price. Price is the *final* value judgment customers make—it is the conclusion they create based on weighing *all* of the benefits a product or brand seems to offer. They make that assessment and then make a comparative price valuation between competing brands. What is usually missed by marketers is that emotional needs are what customers most wish to have satisfied. They will pay significantly more for products that accomplish that for them.

---

## Rule #3: Drive expectations.

---

Before any brand can create Alpha influence, it must drive expectations. This means that it must differentiate itself not by what it does, but by what it makes customers *want*. If it can satisfy those things better than anyone else and at a higher level of emotional needs satisfaction, it then generates controlling influence with customers and competitors. Driving expectations toward higher-level emotional needs automatically pushes the drivers of decisions in your category from lower-level drivers to higher-level ones, so more profitability and greater influence are achieved. (See Chapter 3 for a detailed discussion of drivers of decisions.)

When you attempt to drive expectations on the basis of functionality alone, weak influence is created. When you drive expectations that are emotional (in other words, self-satisfaction and personal significance), your influence is much stronger.

This battle of driving expectations toward higher-level drivers of decisions is the tactical level of the war, whereas the battle of Core Alpha Assets is the strategic one (see Chapter 4). The company that can drive expectations to the highest level has the greatest immediate influence in the marketplace. The longevity of that influence will be based on how strong the company's Core Alpha Asset is compared to others and how well it is proven through Supporting Alpha Assets. But the first battleground for creating change in the category is through driving expectations.

In every company that we helped grow more than 25 percent in a short period of time, we used the method of driving new expectations among customers, distributors, and/or referral agents. The more of those groups we affected, or the more change we created in expectations for any one of those groups, the greater the resulting growth.

Sometimes driving new expectations included product innovation. More often it was focused on creating the *impression* of innovation, while driving a perception that self-satisfaction and personal significance were being enhanced. For instance, one of the food brands we helped move from being a scavenger brand to Alpha status in three months was accomplished solely by changing expectations and satisfying emotional needs, with no change to product or packaging at all. We discussed this ice cream brand in earlier chapters. On the consumer level, this brand created an expectation of homemade taste by re-creating childhood memories that were satisfied totally in the customer's mind. It also created a new level of expectations among its retailers for how a brand could partner with its distribution network by generating more traffic for them *without* having to use discounting to drive that traffic. It set new levels of emotional satisfaction for retailer buyers and upper management.

---

## Rule #4: Measure *causes* over outcomes.

---

Measuring and comparing sales, profit, market share, brand awareness, stock price, margins, or any of the other outcomes that businesses spend so much time worrying over only clouds the focus on the *causes* that drive those desired outcomes. It is critical to create measurements for the causes that are driving changes in outcomes. It is far more productive to understand your company's performance in terms of perceived satisfaction of needs (especially self-satisfaction and personal significance) than in terms of final outcomes. Measuring outcomes alone is like eating a meal without being aware of what you ate and then trying to figure out what might have given you an upset stomach.

Measuring causes is a matter of understanding the 19 sets of possible Supporting Alpha Assets, which are a comprehensive list of potential causal factors, and then measuring those that are at work in your category versus those that are not. (See Chapter 4 for a discussion on Supporting Alpha Assets.) In analyzing the results, you know you have spotted an area of potential weakness when one of those factors is not "active"—meaning that customers are not using that factor to make buying decisions. The more of these Supporting Alpha Assets that are being used to drive decisions, the more control is possible. It's like having extra fetures on your car to make it go fast, letting you adjust tire pressure, turbo boost, air flow, and wind resistance in addition to just stepping on the gas pedal.

For those Supporting Alpha Assets that are active, you need to measure not only how well you are performing with your customers versus how your competitors are performing with theirs, but also how *noncustomers* believe you are performing with your customers. Noncustomers are, after all, your potential new customers, and what they believe about how you satisfy your customers is critical to getting them to consider you or your product.

The beauty of measuring causal factors rather than just measuring outcomes is that you can spot positive or negative changes earlier and therefore make corrections to improve your final outcomes. If I measure the changes in customer perceptions about how well my company is performing in the small things that contribute to their final conclusion that my product is worth purchasing, I have a much earlier opportunity to make changes in what I am doing. These changes can drive much stronger final outcomes, because those outcomes were driven by stronger demand having been created.

Measure causal factors, and you have a chance to improve far more than you can by just measuring your desired final outcomes.

---

## Rule #5: Critical change occurs once competitors start to follow your lead.

---

The critical change of momentum comes when there is a change in the pattern of competitors following the Alpha. You can gain dramatic revenue increases without ever generating a single follower, but you won't be able to sustain your influence until that following activity occurs.

Remember that this process starts with driving new and higher expectations. Once competitors discover that your customers are influencing customers of *other* products to buy your product because you have set new, higher expectations, those competitors start to follow your lead. Once this happens, you have established a level of influence momentum that can be sustained for as long as you protect the Supporting Alpha Assets that got you there.

In some cases, competitors don't quite know what to do to follow you, so they just fall into price promotion in order to compete. That has much the same effect as following behavior, because it concedes that the lead product is too good to compete against on any level *except* by lowering price. In many cases, where we helped a company change expectations in ways that surprised competitors, those competitors did not react immediately by following our customer's lead. Competitors couldn't quite figure out what was going on, so they simply competed with price promotions. All that did was further reinforce to consumers or end users that our customer's product was the one to buy.

---

## Rule #6: Deep, sustainable strength takes time.

---

Like almost everything else in life, developing deep sustainable strength takes time. Although we proved in our tests that a scavenger brand can become an Alpha in a short period of time, to become sustainable takes much longer. Customers, competitors, distributors, referral agents, and even employees need to become accustomed to seeing that new leader in the leadership role and following its lead. Corporate management also needs to accustom the company's culture to that new lead position. Far too often, companies change the things that drove their success before those things have had a chance to create the self-sustaining level that was possible. Using Alpha learning just to drive short-term sales growth reduces these techniques to little more than one more sales promotion. Alpha learning has the potential to drive self-sustaining success over a long period of time. What starts off as a purposeful strategic initiative takes on a life of its own, with customers driving your future success even more than your own purposeful activities.

Many of the oldest Alphas around today actually did not drive their own rise to the Alpha position. That's why it took most of them far longer than the growth we experienced in our tests. But the same thing that drives their longevity will drive the sustainability of a newer, faster-rising Alpha.

Harley-Davidson became the Alpha in its category despite itself. The company was actually embarrassed about the "wild" customer base that became its Core Alpha Asset. Coca-Cola and John Deere did not make themselves the Alpha; their customers did it for them. In fact, I often wonder whether Coca-Cola even understands what its Core Alpha Asset is, when I see the kind of nonfocused support it gives its brand. Sears, on the other hand, was quite purposeful in developing its Alpha position as the country emerged from World War II.

What these Alphas did very well was maintain and protect their Core Alpha Asset and their Supporting Alpha Assets long enough to make themselves almost invulnerable to competitive pressure. It was only as they forgot what those assets were and allowed them to be compromised or disappear that they lost ground. Sears lost it because they forgot who they were and why people shopped there. Harley-Davidson has gradually been losing it because they haven't figured out how to continue driving expectations toward themselves, as Japanese motorcycles become more and more like Harleys. Coca-Cola just barely continues to have it, because Pepsi gave up after they saw the powerful customer uprising to bring back Classic Coke. Because of the longevity of their reigns as Alpha, each of these companies has had time to correct the errors they made. Even as they made mistakes, they did not see the inevitable results in full, because customer loyalty carries an Alpha sometimes for decades after they have lost the reason they became the Alpha.

Although it was obvious that Sears was on the decline in the late 1970s, the longevity of their reign gave them two more decades before they became a survival brand.

How much time does it take to get to the point? There's just too little data to say with any verifiable certainty, but it seems to take more than five years for new Alphas. In some cases, it may take multiple decades of customer experience to create enough depth of belief in the product or brand to approach self-sustainability. Once a product or brand has reached that point, however, it becomes almost invulnerable.

## WHEN YOU CAN'T BE THE OVERALL ALPHA (NO PROBLEM!)

Even if you don't believe you can ever become the overall category Alpha, don't worry. You have two choices: (1) You can simply increase your Supporting Alpha Assets, moving yourself up the pyramid from scavenger or survival brand to aspiring brand or even from aspiring brand to high-influence brand, or (2) you can make yourself into a mini-Alpha, creating your own subcategory in which you can be the Alpha.

The secret is still the same: Find ways to satisfy self-satisfaction and personal significance needs, drive expectations, and stop competing on the basis of price. In our experiments with companies ranging in size from Fortune 100 to small local businesses, we found that almost any effort to address higher levels of self-satisfaction and personal significance was re-warded with increased sales and greater profitability. Where new expectations were being driven and higher levels of emotional needs were being satisfied, the company began to acquire many of the attributes of Alphas, including less vulnerability to competitive pressure and more control over their distribution network. The more they abandoned price promotion as they drove those new expectations, the more they discovered that they could indeed control their future to a level they had never believed possible before.

Making yourself the Alpha of a subcategory is one of the most effective ways to use this learning without getting immediately squashed by a stronger brand. This process uses basic segmentation theory, looking for niches serving unmet needs within the larger category. It then incorporates Alpha learning to make sure that whatever innovation is used to address those needs includes driving expectations toward higher-level needs *and* both self-satisfaction and personal significance. We've already talked about Ben & Jerry's, a company that accomplished this and eventually became the decision driver for the overall ice cream category.

The mistake most strategic teams make when they think about segmentation strategies is that they don't take into account the need to drive expectations higher in addition to simply satisfying an unmet functional need. Many also only use this segmentation strategy to expand the reach of a current brand into new territory without recognizing the need to match new opportunities with their Core Alpha Asset. If the Core Alpha Asset can't encompass that new segment while driving expectations higher, then either the company should not address that unmet need or they should adapt their Core Alpha Asset to become broader.

> *The secret: Find ways to satisfy self-satisfaction and personal significance needs, drive expectations, and stop competing upon price.*

Detroit's Big Three automakers have run into this problem. They struggle with selling upscale auto brands because their Core Alpha Assets have become that of "medium to low price with just-above-minimum functionality." If their Core Alpha Assets were pushed higher, as Japanese automakers have done, they could encompass both high-end and low-end autos. The Japanese entered the U.S. marketplace with cheap, minimally functional automobiles in order to break the hold that Detroit's Big Three had on car dealerships. It was a small niche that Detroit didn't want to address any longer, because they believed they were making the most desired automobiles in the world. Once the Japanese became established, they immediately started upgrading their Core Alpha Asset to include much higher-level experiences and expectations by adding features and "quality" that bypassed Ford, GM, and Chrysler. They even encouraged their dealers not to negotiate on prices, which only helped enhance the desire to own these cars simply because they were obviously worth more.

Japanese automakers also recognized when it was time to create new, even higher-expectation brands, such as Lexus, Acura, and Infinity, opening another level of experience beyond the limits of their current brands. They were careful to continually make sure that both the higher- and lower-end brands supported the same basic Core Alpha Asset, so that people who knew that Honda makes Acura or that Toyota makes Lexus would not be confused. Mercury and Lincoln never really worked from the 1950s onward, because consumer expectations of Ford could not encompass that range. Lexus is merely a natural extension of what Toyota is already doing. If Toyota were still turning out cheap, minimally functional cars, as it did in the 1970s, then Lexus could never be successful. It would be too great a leap for customers to understand that one manufacturer could turn out both lines of cars.

## SUMMARY

Believe in your company's ability to bypass your competitors without discounting or diminishing the value of your product or brand. Don't limit your own growth potential by thinking that past lack of success dictates your future.

Align everything to support your Core Alpha Asset and to

drive you toward self-sustaining success. Make sure that everything proves the experience you want customers to have when they purchase from you.

As CEO, own your success and help others to do the same. Train your staff and your distribution network to expect the highest levels of success from everything you do.

Satisfy at least minimum functionality, but the maximum in emotional needs. Don't compete on price. Compete instead on generating self-satisfaction and personal significance for your customers, distributors, and referral agents.

Push expectations toward higher-level drivers of purchase decisions, especially self-satisfaction and personal significance.

Measure causes, not just final outcomes. Understand the causes that are driving your success, and your competitors' success, and measure changes in them. Don't wait for final outcomes and then try to guess what caused them. Otherwise, you will always be trying to catch up with yourself and the marketplace.

Watch for the critical change to occur, when competitors start to follow your lead. That signals the major shift that can launch you into an Alpha position, if you notice it and sustain it.

Give success a chance to mature before expecting that newfound influence to sustain you for long despite mistakes and disasters.

Use the Alpha learning to create more income, more profitability, and more control for your company, even if you have no hope of ever becoming the overall Alpha of your category. Even without making yourself the Alpha of a subsegment of the category, you can still generate many Alpha benefits just by addressing satisfaction and significance, and by attempting to drive expectations higher.

# 6

## SPOTTING POTENTIAL ALPHAS

---

Why worry about spotting potential Alphas that are not currently driving significant category expectations? Why even think about competitors that haven't proven themselves immediate threats to you yet? By definition, potential Alphas have the proven ability to become expectation drivers for your product category. That should create concern all by itself. But add to that the fact that, once they become visible, it will probably be too late to stop the damage to your competitive strength, it becomes obvious that you should want to know who they are as early as possible.

How many times have businesses been blindsided by an upstart company that "suddenly" comes out of nowhere and starts drawing customers away from the major players? This happens far more often than any business leader would like to admit. Every business owner or CEO would like to believe that growth potential in a competitor would be obvious early enough that he could take action to overcome it. Far too often, however, it is the very company that was not being taken seriously that somehow becomes a competitive concern.

We discovered that those upstart companies seldom actually come out of "nowhere." They were quietly doing impressive things, while the major players ignored them because of their small market share. Compounding that was the fact that those major players did not recognize the satisfaction and significance strategies being employed by those upstart companies. The result was that the small player gained far more influence than any of the big players ever expected they could, even though they were doing it right in front of the eyes of those major companies.

I recall vividly the first Toyotas and Hondas that began showing up in the United States in the 1970s. They were horrible-looking, cheap little cars (at least to my Americanized, muscle-car eyes). They looked like death traps to me. Even into the early 1980s, the analogy popularly used for an almost total lack of quality was Toyota. The analogy for highest quality was Cadillac. In business meetings you would hear managers refer to a high-quality alternative as the "Cadillac of the industry," while the cut-rate, lowest-quality version was considered the "Toyota of the industry." Ten years later, Cadillac was considered out-of-date, backward-looking, and reserved for old folks who didn't recognize real quality when they saw it. Toyota (and Honda not far behind them) had become the trend leader, pushing consumer expectations far beyond anything that Detroit was turning out.

This phenomenon didn't come out of nowhere. It happened right in front of everyone's eyes. It was just that no one in the Big Three U.S. automakers seemed to recognize it for what it was. While Ford, GM, and Chrysler were making incremental improvements to their vehicles and focusing on new governmental requirements for emissions, safety, and fuel economy, Toyota and Honda were taking the best of European design,

> *Revolutionary new Alphas don't come out of nowhere. They create themselves right in front of everyone's eyes.*

adding as many upscale satisfaction and significance features as they could, and making their cars affordable to middle-class Americans. One of the illustrative battlefronts in this war involved the cup holder. It took at least a decade for U.S. automakers to even join the battle, and by the time they finally added cup holders to their vehicles, Toyota and Honda already had more and better ones in the *backseat* than U.S. autos had in the front.

While Japanese manufacturers innovated for self-satisfaction and personal significance to capture what Mercedes-Benz and BMW had missed or not protected, Detroit imagined that it could continue to get away with providing minimum functionality and minimum emotional needs satisfaction at a reasonable cost and leave it at that. The trouble was that the expectations changed. It wasn't just that big, gas-guzzling vehicles had become "un-American," as people tried to save fuel and lessen our dependence on expensive foreign oil. It was also that people discovered that they could afford the luxuries they had long aspired to own. They could have a little bit of what they imagined a Mercedes offered, but at a price that was only a bit higher than that of an American car.

This might have been spotted earlier if Detroit had known what to look for. If U.S. automakers had been measuring self-satisfaction and personal significance instead of *functional* satisfaction, which was being measured in customer satisfaction surveys, they would have noticed something very frightening: Some competitors were generating a great deal of loyalty among their small customer groups by satisfying higher-level needs. Their influence in the marketplace was growing quickly, and the result was that other competitors were starting to follow their lead rather than the lead of U.S. automakers. By the early 1990s, U.S. automakers had become such devoted followers of Japanese autos that they were styling their cars after them and adding features that Japanese cars had offered the previous year.

Detroit actually started getting worried in the 1980s, but their reaction was not to recognize the problem but, rather, to focus on *quality* improvement. They even sent their plant people to Japan to learn how Japanese plants worked. Yes, Japanese manufacturers were doing a better job of controlling the manufacturing process by using robotics, computerized machine tools, and better management practices, but these were not what drove the success of Japanese autos. The reason for their success was that they recognized the satisfaction and significance factors that could make them the expectation leaders. My guess is, however, that they never expected U.S. automakers to be so blind to what they were doing, giving them a multiple-decade head start.

> *First, forget share or brand visibility (brand awareness) as primary indicators.*

Ben & Jerry's certainly didn't just appear and become the Alpha of the ice cream category. The company had been around for many years, doing silly, quirky things, such as loading their ice cream with lots of goodies, before their impact on customer expectations became so great that most competitors started to follow their lead. They had to work hard to get there, but in the meantime the other major brands pretty much ignored them as upstarts that could not affect their business. Even after Ben & Jerry's had clearly become the expectation leader among superpremium brands, regular premium ice cream manufacturers continued to ignore them. They considered Ben & Jerry's a niche brand that would not have an effect on them. Soon enough, however, in boardrooms throughout the frozen dessert industry, executives were wondering how they could take advantage of the "new trend" toward more stuff in ice cream.

Spotting potential Alphas is far from easy. None of the traditional measurements reveal them until it was far too late to do anything about it. First, forget share or brand visibility (also called "brand awareness") as primary indicators. Even though these are almost always the first things asked for in a market analysis, they are not indicators of long-term, sustainable success. Remember that just because a brand has been able to gain share or brand visibility in the past, that is no predictor that it will be able to maintain it in the future. That's especially true when a leading-share brand has created or maintained its market share based on functional needs satisfaction or pricing. There are far too many examples of "leading" brands that have been eclipsed by seeming newcomers who come out of "nowhere" to steal customers and market share by offering better functional performance or lower pricing.

> *Past performance is no predictor of future success . . . Higher influence generated through satisfaction and significance fulfillment is.*

In fact, the moment a company starts to think it is safe because of its past success, it is actually in trouble. Too many companies that were once very successful missed the signs of their own demise in the same way they missed the rise of new competitors. I recall several meetings among top Sears executives where questions about the corporate direction and the growth of Kmart were dismissed with a comment to the effect of, "We're the biggest retailer in history. We must be the best and the smartest." In less than a decade, Kmart more than doubled its market share, threatening Sears' hold on middle-class America. Then Kmart, in turn, lost sight of its vulnerabilities by focusing on its past successes and not recognizing that the changes it was making were disastrous, as Wal-Mart took the lead position. The only way to avoid this same fate is to stop looking back at past success and start looking forward to changes that are driving new and higher-level expectations.

Instead of looking at share or brand visibility, look at the amount of loyalty that is being generated among current customers. Even if there are not a lot of those customers yet, they may have enough influence to affect decisions of customers of other brands in the category. I would much rather have a brand with a few influential customers who are so loyal that they can drive customers of other brands to change their buying habits than have a currently high-share brand with customers who keep their "satisfaction" to themselves.

We've been able to spot many potential Alphas that eventually grew to become extremely influential by measuring the amount of loyalty they generated through the fulfillment of self-satisfaction and personal significance needs. One such case concerned an ice cream brand in the Pittsburgh region.

One of our customers had just purchased a seemingly strong regional brand there. It had been the top brand for more than a decade, with more than double the market share of its nearest competitor, primarily using buy-one-get-one-free offers to drive demand. All major competitors followed their lead and competed by offering buy-one-get-one-free sales. As we assessed the category for the new owners, we spotted a brand that showed significantly more influence through satisfaction and significance fulfillment—at least within its smaller customer base. It was number three in the market, with less than half the market share of our customer's newly acquired brand.

When our customer saw this, they immediately contacted every one of their retailers, distributors and brokers, and salespeople to ask whether any of them believed this upstart brand had a chance of rolling over their newly acquired top brand. Without exception, none of these sources of market insight believed this lesser brand had a chance to overcome the juggernaut of the number one brand. Unfortunately, within one year that lesser brand, Edy's, had not only grown but had become number one, taking most of its share growth from our customer's new brand.

It was a simple matter of being blinded by the belief that what happened yesterday or today is what you can expect tomorrow. The truth is that past performance is no predictor of future success. Higher influence generated through satisfaction and significance fulfillment is.

That's the problem with backward-looking market analysis. If you believe you can project forward a trend based on past activity, you risk missing the really big factors that can change everything in a category. It's like driving a car by looking out the back window. As long as the road continues straight ahead and no one comes in from a side road, you can go along very well for some time. But any major change lurking on the road ahead can't be anticipated, and it could spell either disaster or a rough detour.

> *Spotting potential Alphas requires a complete change in how you look at markets.*

Spotting potential Alphas requires a complete change in how you look at markets. You have to look forward, not backward. You have to be watching for those companies, products, or brands that are *starting* to generate influential loyalty among their small customer group, using satisfaction and significance fulfillment to drive it. Backward-looking analysis misses that, because the trend is not clear enough in the early stages of a potential Alpha's development, when a more influential brand still has the chance to overcome the threat.

Another customer of ours had us do a market analysis about three years ago. They are the top market share brand in their category and have been for decades. They were most interested in opportunities for growing the category overall and for reinforcing their Supporting Alpha Assets to make sure they remained top dog in the category.

In the analysis, we spotted a smaller, niche brand that was generating a great deal of loyalty among their smaller customer base. We brought our customer's attention to the brand, but ended up having a long discussion with their marketing team, who did not believe this niche brand was a serious player. Some of their staff got pretty upset at the idea that such a small brand should even be considered a strategic threat. A few months ago, I attended a meeting with them and listened as several staff members noted that this once smaller brand was beginning to "show up everywhere," gaining distribution and shelf space in places they never expected to see it. It was also expanding its influence into other segments of the overall category. Suddenly, this niche player was looking like a serious threat.

How quickly a potential Alpha can fulfill that potential depends on many factors. The first and probably most important factor is whether or not the management team has the desire to grow the company into a leading role or has recognized what it will take to make that happen. Obviously, a corporate team that doesn't want to grow their business into a leading role can easily undermine any strength the company, product, or brand has. From an acquisition standpoint, this opportunity is about as good as it gets—a product, brand, or company with the potential to become an Alpha, yet the management team doesn't recognize that potential.

Probably the second most important factor in driving the speed of change is an influential customer or referral agent base. For some products, like chewing gum, that are purchased often and shared with friends, the influence of passionate loyalty to one brand or product is potentially very contagious. In other categories, where product is either purchased less often or not shared with others as often, the influence of the customers or referral agents might have to be much higher. For instance, the turnaround of U.S. Savings Bonds benefited from having financial writers and knowledgeable investors recommend the new I Bond product, which drove acceptance from less-knowledgeable potential customers. These were the same referral agents who had worked against the product earlier but now became advocates for the revamped U.S. Savings Bond.

For a fish food product we worked on, the greatest influence came from both retail salespersons and very knowledgeable, experienced aquarium hobbyists who held great sway with beginning hobbyists. When both of these groups believed in a product, it almost *had* to grow. Understanding the influence of the customer groups being reached by a potential new Alpha can help predict how quickly it might grow to its potential.

The final big factor that can help predict the speed with which change can occur is how much competitive activity is currently going on in the category. The more marketing communication that is taking place, the more potential customers are hearing and thinking about the category. That works to the benefit of those with higher influence, but it also allows a potential Alpha that is just starting to take its strong niche influence to the larger category to grow much faster than it might have otherwise. Quiet categories slow the growth for everyone in a category.

## KEY COMPONENTS THAT HELP PREDICT HOW QUICKLY A PRODUCT WITH HIGH INFLUENCE CAN GROW:

- Management that wants growth and recognizes the real strengths their company has that are driving their influence
- A customer base that is influential with other customer groups (becoming referral agents)
- How often the product is purchased and shared with others
- How respected customers are among less-knowledgeable buyers in the category
- The amount of competitive activity
- How much competitive marketing communication is going on
- How many competitors there are (the more, the better in a high-communication market)

So what can you do once you've spotted a potential Alpha? The first thing you can do is learn from them. Don't waste your time trying to copy their products or services, but do try to understand how they are influencing customers, distribution networks, and referral agents. The answer will always come back to what they are doing to generate self-satisfaction and personal significance. What you will certainly learn is more about how customers in your category *want* to be making decisions, because, as we discussed earlier, people will always move toward higher-level needs satisfaction when given the chance. Determine whether they are driving new expectations or simply addressing ones that were already being addressed, but doing it better. New expectations indicate an important change in direction for the category, while simply doing a better job of addressing current ones doesn't.

> *The first and probably most important factor driving speed of change is whether or not the management team has the desire to grow.*

The second thing you can do is determine whether you can incorporate what they are doing, and make it your own. Certainly the first rule of strategic competition is not to copy your competitor. But if you are already significantly more influential with a broader set of customers than the potential Alpha, you may be able to take what they do well and make it your own. Of course, that depends on whether you can accomplish that while they are still simply a niche brand and *not* after they have already started to influence the larger category. Microsoft has done that for years. Microsoft's innovation has more often than not just been a matter of taking what others are already doing well and creating their own version of it.

Third, you can innovate past the potential Alpha. Once you understand the level of self-satisfaction and personal significance they are addressing, you may be able to innovate to address even higher levels. Shooting higher always gives you more potential for greater influence. If they are starting to drive new expectations and you are already influential enough in your category, you may be able to take those new expectations and make them the ones customers expect from you. Or you may wish to guide expectations into a new direction based on other innovation you have been working to develop.

Last, you could seek to acquire them. Although most potential Alphas we've spotted are subbrands of larger companies that don't recognize them for what they are, there may be an opportunity to truly make their strengths your own. If managed well (meaning not just acquiring them for non–Alpha Factor reasons), the strengths that make them a potential Alpha could dovetail with your own to make you even more influential in the marketplace.

## SUMMARY

If you can learn to spot potential Alphas, you can prepare your company not to become one of their followers. If you are already more influential than they, you can either take what they "own" and make it yours or innovate beyond them. Far too much investment is wasted by competing with products, companies, and brands that aren't worth it. Every aspiring Alpha must learn to recognize who his real competitors are.

As an outsider, you can predict who has the potential for significant change in share and future profitability. This also makes spotting potential Alphas great acquisition ground. More often than not, potential Alphas don't even know they are so close to becoming influentially powerful in their category. Buy one early, and you can make its strength part of your own, making your Alpha Assets even more formidable.

Once you spot a potential Alpha, you have many choices of what to do with that knowledge, depending on how influential you already are. You can simply observe them to discover what they have learned about addressing higher-level needs for satisfaction and significance. You can possibly make the expectations they are addressing your own, so that they become secondary to you. You can innovate past them, addressing even higher-level satisfaction and significance needs, thereby driving new expectations. Or you can acquire them and make your own influence even stronger.

## SECTION 3:
## THE BIG "AH-HA'S"

Here are some of the biggest
surprises that came out of the
Alpha Factor Project.

# BIG AH-HA #1: YOU DON'T HAVE TO BE THE BIGGEST TO DOMINATE DECISIONS IN YOUR CATEGORY.

*Non-Alpha thinking*: "Size (market share, number of employees, number of locations) equals domination."

Often a smaller competitor in the category is the real Alpha. When this is the case, the largest brand is so focused on competition that it is not leading at all, but following—often it is following many other competitors in an attempt to keep ahead of them. A good example of this phenomenon is Ben & Jerry's ice cream. When we were doing a lot of work in the ice cream industry, Ben & Jerry's had about half the dollar share of the category leader, Breyers, and later Edy's/Dreyer's.

Ben & Jerry's however, was the true Alpha of the category. It was the brand that was driving expectations of ice cream customers by offering more and bigger pieces of nuts, fruit, and candy mixed in to the ice cream, as well as exotic flavors. Its influence eventually forced almost every other competitor to start following its lead. Now almost every brand, including store brands, competes on over-the-top flavors. Until Ben & Jerry's management changed, no other competitor could come close to the influence the brand had on customer, retailer, and distributor expectations. It was the first choice in super-premium ice cream, drove category expectations, and, therefore, had the highest price leverage among even super-premium brands. It regularly retailed for anywhere from 4 to 12 times the price of "regular" ice cream.

> *Size is only an outcome of doing something better than someone else* in the past. *It doesn't reflect future potential.*

I'm always a bit surprised that, in this day of small upstart companies doing amazing innovation and the all-too-public problems of some of the biggest organizations in the world, there are still those who believe that if you're really big, you must be really good. That has never been true and never will be. Many of the largest organizations in the world are, in fact, very good at what they do and what they offer. They really could not sustain their size for many decades otherwise, but size has never correlated directly with long-term success potential. Size is an outcome of doing something better than someone else *in the past.* We are concerned about the future here, and predicting future success has nothing to do with current size, share, profitability, or any other final outcome that can be measured. It has to do with how willing and how savvy the organization is at driving expectations and thereby creating a new future.

You can learn more about predicting future success for your company and for your competitors on The Alpha Factor website (*www.thealphafactor.com*). There are a number of tools discussed there that can predict future success and can help uncover methods for overcoming much larger competitors.

# BIG AH-HA #2: PRICE IS THE LAST DECISION CRITERIA APPLIED, NOT THE FIRST.

*Non-Alpha thinking:* "Price is everything."

Price is not the comparison, unless there is nothing else of value to compare.

What's the first thing a salesperson will say is driving their marketing success or failure? It's price, right? That's what their buyers typically told them made the difference, no matter what the *real* cause was. Price is also the first thing a consumer will typically say was the deciding factor for a purchase.

We discovered that there are two reasons that we regularly hear price as the deciding factor. The first is a lack of differentiation—customers saw no difference of any value between the higher-priced options and what they purchased. The second is that they either did not fully understand *why* they made the decision or they did not wish to *reveal* the actual reasons in order to avoid conflict or because of embarrassment. In our research, when customers were pushed to really analyze the process they followed in making a decision, price was the *last* thing they considered. Price is the ultimate value *conclusion*, not the decision factor.

If price truly were everything, there would be no Mercedes-

Benz, BMW, Porsche, Ferrari, Etiene Aignier, Christian Dior, Harley-Davidson, Victoria's Secret, Godiva Chocolate, Tiffany's, Rolex, Häagen Dazs, Ben & Jerry's, Dom Perignon, Ethan Allen . . . we could continue this list for pages, but I'm sure you get the point. People prove every day that they are willing to pay more for something they believe gives them more. Yet when you talk to a marketer, the first objection they typically have is, "But in my industry, price really *is* everything." That is true only because they have been made to believe that price is the critical factor and they work hard to prove it to themselves.

> *Price is the ultimate value conclusion, not the decision factor. People prove every day that they are willing to pay more for something they believe gives them "more."*

It takes a lot of work to believe that it all comes down to price. You have to ignore the fact that someone else in your industry is getting a higher price for their products than you are. Not everyone can be the lowest-priced provider, so every competitor except one is getting more money for their products. You also have to ignore the fact that your customers are really saying that your products or services are not different enough from everyone else's to justify a higher price. And then you have to ignore the fact that every distributor's buyer who tells you that you are priced too high is paid to get you to lower your price, no matter what your product is really worth.

Consumers are not really interested in buying the least expensive thing. What they really want is something that satisfies a functional need and makes them feel smarter, more attractive, more admired, more self-satisfied, more significant. We did a huge, multiyear coupon usage study as part of the Alpha Factor Project. What we discovered was pretty depressing for the thousands of companies that spend millions of dollars every month on coupons. Only about 10 percent of the population even said they used coupons "every chance they got." More than 90 percent of all coupons were used by people who said they would have purchased the product at the regular price anyway.

Even for trial of new products, the largest percentage of people said they would wait for a personal recommendation before they would buy the product. Then they would buy it at regular price, *if* no coupon was available. Price was not the deciding factor.

As we explored the decision process throughout this project, we discovered that price was the *last* thing customers considered. Everything else took precedence. Only after exhausting every other possibility for driving a preference did price become the deciding factor.

Salespeople are notorious for hearing that the reason they lost a sale was price. You can almost count on that being the stated reason they lost the sale. It wasn't the product. It certainly wasn't anything they did. What they heard was "price" as the deciding factor.

I found myself telling a salesperson just the other day that the reason I chose another product was because I got it cheaper somewhere else. I said that not because it was true, but because I knew he would accept it without my having to get into an argument about the value judgments I made in comparing the products I considered. I was a bit embarrassed after the phone call, but I was certain that he was not going to make it easy on me, even though there was no hope of his getting the sale.

As long as you believe that price is going to be the deciding factor in a buying decision, you are admitting either that you have nothing of value to offer or that you want to take the easy way out and ignore the truth. Discover the secret to overcoming price by visiting The Alpha Factor website (*www.thealphafactor.com*). By understanding the essential elements of The Alpha Factor, you can actually make someone else's lower price *increase* your product's value.

---

# BIG AH-HA #3: YOU DON'T HAVE TO BE THE FIRST TO MARKET WITH AN IDEA TO BE THE DOMINANT MARKETER OF IT.

---

*Non-Alpha thinking*: "First in the game runs the game."

The first one to market has the advantage only until someone with some real understanding of needs satisfaction shows up.

Few of the top marketers today were either the first in the category or the first with the type of product they currently sell. It is actually more noteworthy when someone who *was* the first becomes the top brand and can maintain that for any time. Softsoap is one of the rare examples. I was amazed to watch them go from being first in the category to top brand despite pressure from marketing behemoths in the packaged-goods industry. I was even more surprised to see Softsoap maintain its strength for many years after it was sold to Colgate-Palmolive, since large companies often kill the very Supporting Alpha Assets that created the success for the acquired brand.

Starbucks did not create the high-end coffee shop. Nor did they have a corner on great coffee. In fact, when a customer of mine and I were scouting the opportunity for starting a coffee shop chain in Virginia, we went to San Francisco where there was almost one coffee shop at every intersection in the city. Most served better coffee than Starbucks.

Victoria's Secret did not create sexy underwear, nor were they first to market it. Frederick's of Hollywood had been offering such things for decades before Victoria's Secret ever showed up. Victoria's Secret just marketed it in a more socially acceptable way.

> *Few of the top marketers today were either the first in their category or the first with the type of product they currently sell.*

Harley-Davidson did not create the motorcycle, multicylinder engines, the V-twin, or even the famous Harley sound. That sound was created by Harley customizers. Harley-Davidson just capitalized on a mind-set, attitude, and lifestyle that were extremely attractive to baby boomers who came of age in the 1960s.

Microsoft did not create the DOS operating system; they just used it to create a platform for hundreds of arguably second-rate software programs and gained instant distribution by making it the platform of choice on IBM PCs. It also was not the first to market with a great word-processing program or spreadsheet. They have most typically played catch-up to other better products throughout their entire existence.

Sears was not the largest retailer in the world, because they were the *first* general merchandise retailer. They also weren't the first to do store-brand products. What Sears may have been the first to do was Basic Buying. Basic Buying was what Sears called their process of custom-designing a line of products from the ground up, contracting their manufacture, and then applying their own brand names to them. What really made Sears the largest retailer at the end of World War II were three things: (1) the Basic Buying concept, (2) offering a "good, better, best" trade-up of products in a line, ranging from an extremely affordable opening price point to Sears Best, and (3) being the first retailer to offer credit to newly married couples.

Even though Armstrong was the dominant brand in no-wax resilient flooring for decades, they were not the first to market with a low-maintenance floor. What made Armstrong the king of interior decorating with flooring, carpets, and ceilings was an image they created for themselves as the most knowledgeable resource for ideas about interior design and home lifestyle. Their single greatest asset was the monthly advertising they did in all of the top shelter magazines, such as *Better Homes and Gardens.* They had long-term renewable contracts for the inside front spread in all the top home magazines every month. It made them the brand of choice in a category with many domestic and foreign competitors. They even started a catalog to sell the decorator items that they showed in their ads, because so many people wrote or called to find out where they could get those items. Although they made some dramatic mistakes through the years, such as believing that they had to compete with other brands, the thing that really killed the Armstrong brand was when they stopped renewing those ad contracts and gave away their leading image.

If you visit The Alpha Factor website (*www.thealphafactor*

*.com*), you can learn much more about satisfying higher-level needs to create dominance, even if you are the last to enter the market.

## BIG AH-HA #4: YOU DON'T HAVE TO HAVE THE HIGHEST QUALITY TO BE THE DOMINANT PLAYER.

*Non-Alpha thinking*: "Best quality is what the customer wants."

Entire service industries have been created around the false assumption that customers want the highest quality. They facilitate innovation and process controls to increase quality, when most of these marketers have little, if any, proof that quality is the key motivator of purchases—or even *could* be the key motivator. The TQM (Total Quality Management) fad and the Six Sigma focus of so many marketers are direct outcomes of this thinking.

Every motorcycle owner knows that Harley-Davidsons are far from being the best-quality product in the category. Japanese bikes hold that position, although they have not been able to generate either the price leverage or the brand loyalty among any but a small segment of buyers.

American autos may have had a brief period after World War II of being good-quality products, but they held on to their sales lead in the United States long after they had lost the quality battle to the Japanese and the Europeans. It has only been since American auto manufacturers lost all sight of what Americans even want to purchase in a car that they have abdicated share to the Japanese. Today, the issue in autos is less about quality, which is high among almost all automotive products, but rather about styling, self-satisfaction, and significance. Ask young people today if they'd rather have a Toyota or a Ford, and you will get an overwhelming response in favor of Toyota. Even pickup trucks are moving away from U.S. automakers toward the Japanese, because they know what ego satisfaction features to add to their vehicles to drive demand. You have to work hard to convince yourself to want an American car these days.

> *Entire service industries have been created around the false assumption that customers want the highest quality.*

Designer clothes are notorious for being of lower quality than many other brands, but they provide an ego stroke that Kmart or Wal-Mart just can't match.

Quality is a "soft" conclusion that is easily swayed in its importance to the decision process. Quality, like value, is a *conclusion* drawn from an assessment of many other decision factors being weighed and considered. A few marketers have made quality the differentiating factor for themselves, whether their quality is really the best or not.

Here are two examples:

L.L. Bean has an unconditional lifetime warranty on its

backpacks that has made it the number one choice among parents of grade-school children. Are its products really of better quality? That's debatable, but the trust generated by their focus on making customers feel smart when they buy from L.L. Bean pays off.

Sears' Craftsman hand tools, with their unconditional lifetime warranty, were once the tool of choice among most homeowners and many professionals. I recall an article about a thief who said that he always stole Craftsman tools because he could always get them replaced free if he broke one.

The Alpha Factor website (*www.thealphafactor.com*) is a great place to start, if you want to discover tools that can help you innovate to overcome a competitor's higher quality product and yet make your product a better "value" in their minds.

---

## BIG AH-HA #5: PERCEPTIONS DRIVE DECISIONS—NOT THE "HARD" FACTORS YOU BELIEVE MIGHT.

---

*Non-Alpha thinking*: "Manage the 'hard' stuff and success will follow."

This is probably the easiest to accept of all the big Ah-ha's. We've been hearing for decades that "perception is everything." The problem with that is that it usually means, "Make people believe a lie, and it becomes the truth." That is most certainly *not* true in marketing and revenue generation—at least not over the long term.

What *is* true is that the perceptions people have about your brand, your product, your people, your distribution, and just about everything else about your company drive (1) their expectations, (2) their predisposition to consider what you offer, and (3) their trust in you. But those perceptions have to be proven by the "hard" stuff—product, distribution, customer service, and so on—to make them true.

Customers are really tough on marketers who do not back up with hard proof the perceptions they *wish* customers to have. Emerging Alphas know who they are and what they want people to think about them. They have the strongest, highest-level Core Alpha Asset in their category (see Chapter 4 for an explanation of Core Alpha Assets). Then they prove those things through everything they do. This total commitment to proving their Core Alpha Asset is something that differentiates growing Alphas from almost everyone else.

Too often in the Alpha Factor Project we witnessed companies that said one thing and then acted quite differently. For instance, how many banks have advertising campaigns that say they "listen" to customer needs? I see such claims all the time. Yet very few actually do listen. In fact, many years of work in banking and financial services showed us that the biggest complaint about banks by customers is that they *don't* listen and they *don't* care about customer needs. That kind of disconnect between perception and reality is not overcome by empty claims or clever advertising. It can be overcome only by actually listening and actually caring. It has to be proven in everything they do, not just in what they say.

So what do you do if you haven't been able to create strong perceptions about your product, brand, or company? That's actually about the most ideal situation to start a run for the Alpha position. You have a clean slate and can create whatever will generate the greatest growth.

Start with an assessment of what the real key drivers are in your category—not the ones customers are currently using to make purchase decisions, but the ones that customers *wish* they could be using. When customers say that "price" or "retail salesperson recommendation" or "availability" is the key driver of decisions, find out whether they would not rather be making decisions based on higher emotional needs satisfaction. For instance, wouldn't they rather prefer to buy the product that is "best" in the category, or the one that they believe smarter people purchase, or the one that they believe will make others think they are smarter or more admirable for having purchased it? Seek out what the unmet needs are that they believe aren't being addressed or can't be addressed. You will discover a whole set of things that almost any marketer could use to drive expectations higher and gain control over the category. If you then use these to prove a Core Alpha Asset that is higher and stronger than those of competitors, you can quickly become a leading innovator in your category.

*Negative perceptions can be overcome. customers are less concerned about carrying a grudge for past failures than they are about finding someone who will address higher-level emotional needs.*

What if you have a truly negative perception? Change it. Customers truly have a short memory, when you learn how to do things right. First Union Bank, one of the largest banks ever to exist in the United States, did such a terrible job of caring for their customers that they had to buy another much smaller bank with a better reputation and then change First Union's name to Wachovia. To prove that they had learned something, they also worked hard to change the things that had gotten them into trouble in the first place. Negative perceptions can be overcome, because customers are less concerned about carrying a grudge for past failures than they are about finding someone who will address higher-level emotional needs for them. Customers can be very forgiving, when they see you moving toward satisfaction and significance fulfillment.

Sometimes it's just a matter of finding a new way to prove the underlying strong perceptions about the organization that were fogged by a bad product or market approach. One thing that surprised me about our experience with the U.S. Department of the Treasury's Savings Bond program was that the Series E Bonds had such a bad reputation among financial writers and even among their customers, yet they were able to turn around their sales decline quickly. By creating the I Bond, a new product indexed to inflation, which is a basic fear of investors, they made purchasers and financial writers feel much smarter for buying and recommending the product. Whereas U.S. Savings Bonds were once called "the worst financial product in America," the I Bond was considered a "wise, safe investment choice," even though it still offered lower interest than many other investment options. What allowed that change was the core perception of the U.S. Department of the Treasury as the most secure financial institution in the world.

For another large organization that had a product with a similarly negative perception, we had to start from scratch. The existing product had no hope of growing within the perception of what people believed the organization did, so we helped them discover and create an entirely new business opportunity using their existing capabilities. Here again, the new business opportunity existed only because the core perception of the organization was positive. It was just the specific product they wanted to grow that was the problem.

Perception is critical, but the Alpha Factor Project learning showed that you can modify and create new, stronger perceptions by understanding what customers really want to be offered instead of just trusting that the market has already defined that and is already addressing it.

The Alpha Factor website (*www.thealphafactor.com*) can help you understand even more about how you can drive perceptions and expectations to your benefit. You will find several tools designed specifically to understand the real drivers of decisions that customers *wish* were at work in your category.

## BIG AH-HA #6: YOU CAN PREDICT WHO WILL GROW DRAMATICALLY BEFORE THAT GROWTH EVEN STARTS.

*Non-Alpha thinking*: "The past predicts the future."

It is indeed impossible to predict growth before it starts by looking at traditional measurement factors. That's because all those traditional measurements are *outcomes*, not *causes*. Outcome measurements look backward at the results of past activity, not forward at the causes of future outcomes. It only makes sense that if you can define and measure the causal factors that will drive those future outcomes, you can predict growth for those organizations that are performing well in those causal factors.

We discovered 19 sets of causal factors that can be measured, all of which are indicators of perceptions and current performance and have the potential of driving large-scale future changes in buying habits. These 19 sets of factors fall into four general categories: Differentiation, Loyalty Generation, Needs Satisfaction, and Communications Effectiveness. (See Chapter 4 for a complete list of Supporting Alpha Assets.) They were almost universal in application. There were only a few that did not apply to every category we tested, including both consumer and commercial/industrial products and services.

By comparing performance of all competitors in your category in these factors, you start to get a picture of who really is creating future growth potential and who isn't. By going further and comparing performance in these factors against customer expectations, you get an even clearer picture of who is overdelivering in unimportant areas, such as price, selection, and even product performance, and who is underdelivering on really critical factors, such as emotional needs. Often we see the most telling indicators by understanding customer willingness to pay more for a specific product, their willingness to go out of their way to find it, and their resistance to buying competitive products even when their first choice is not available. Products or brands that have generated that kind of loyalty, even within a small segment of the market, need to be watched. And if that product's customers are influential with customers of other products (due to experience or status), then the situation really needs to be watched carefully.

> *Products or brands that have generated Alpha-style loyalty, even amongst a small segment of the market, need to be watched.*

As discussed in Chapter 6, using these 19 sets of factors, we have been able to predict many unforeseen changes in market share. Businesses on the verge of growing significantly always reveal themselves in causal factors that drive higher expectations and fulfill higher-level needs, such as self-satisfaction and personal significance.

Don't be blinded to their potential just because they have not yet realized the final outcomes of increased market share or greater distribution. Those outcomes are the *result* of performing at higher levels in the 19 Supporting Alpha Asset factors.

Would you like to find some tools that can predict your success and the potential success of your competitors? The Alpha Factor website (*www.thealphafactor.com*) can get you started in understanding how you can become both a predictor and creator of future success.

## BIG AH-HA #7: MEASURING FINAL OUTCOMES OFTEN BLINDS ONE TO THE CAUSES THAT DRIVE THEM.

*Non-Alpha thinking*: "Focusing on final outcomes is critical to driving and maintaining success."

Outcome measurement is the mainstay of corporate management and traditional marketing research—return on investment, bottom-line profit, sales, direct costs, overhead, market share, brand awareness, penetration of available distribution, end-user predisposition to buy, customer satisfaction, and on and on goes the list. All are outcomes, not drivers of decisions (or causal factors) that lead to those outcomes.

The analysis of how to affect those outcomes is most typically done in conference rooms by *guessing* what has been causing them. I've sat at too many boardroom tables and listened to internal managers brainstorm about why outcomes are what they are without any real basis for those judgments other than personal opinion. Even research that is intended to delve into causes often ignores the fact that people may not be able to tell you directly what caused them to make the decision they did.

It is imperative to discover and measure the real causes that are driving decisions. Otherwise, it is easy to become blinded to these causes. When this happens, corporate teams develop their own list of causal factors, believing wholeheartedly in them, and they attribute everything that happens from that point on to factors on that list. Since there is no new insight being provided into actual causes, they simply continue to attribute everything to those factors, no matter how misguided they are.

> *The secret to understanding causal factors is to assess core drivers of decisions – the reasons that go beyond the superficial stated reasons, uncovering instead the root emotional factors that drove the value judgment.*

The secret to success in understanding causal factors is to continually be assessing actual core drivers of decisions—the reasons that go beyond the obvious and superficial stated reasons given, uncovering instead the root emotional factors that drove the value judgment that was made. And there are multiple levels to that judgment. When a person says that he made a decision based on something being a better value or having a lower price than something else, you are hearing only the most superficial level of judgment. It is a conclusion, not a driver.

When someone goes deeper and lists the features or specific services that made one product seem a better value, again you are hearing conclusions. At the real core is an emotional judgment that says, "I will feel more self-satisfied and/or more significant buying this product compared to others I have seen." Until you get to that point, all you are hearing is a list of features that seem to prove that there will be a more fulfilling experience if you purchase that product.

Why isn't just knowing that enough? Because if you simply develop a list of features and services that are driving value judgments, you are very likely to miss the opportunities that can drive significant changes in expectations. And if a competitor discovers those change drivers first, you may quickly find your products being outclassed and outpaced. You must continually be monitoring customers' belief that they will have their emotional needs fulfilled by using a product in your category. As that belief changes over time, and as competitors try to change expectations either through product innovation or through other means, you must be able to track those changes in order to spot future opportunities.

Simply measuring final outcomes blinds you to any of this change until it has already passed you by, leaving you in a defensive, catch-up position. You must understand how—and if—emotional needs are being fulfilled by you and your competitors, tracking changes in how customers expect these needs to be fulfilled, and you will have the key to truly understanding the strategic drivers of decisions in your category.

Alpha Factor tools discussed on The Alpha Factor website (*www.thealphafactor.com*) give you a number of options for digging beyond final outcomes to discover the real drivers of decisions. In fact, there are tools discussed there that allow you to test new ways to drive stronger value judgments for your product or service.

# BIG AH-HA #8: COMPETITION IS DESIRABLE, BECAUSE IT CAN BE CONTROLLED TO SUPPORT YOU.

*Non-Alpha thinking*: "Competition should be eliminated and attacked."

We all know that the fundamental concept in capitalism is that competition creates improvements that would otherwise not occur. But what we discovered is even more significant: Competitors can be your best marketing support mechanism.

Most top managers either openly or secretly wish they could eliminate all competition. They see competitors as limiters, who make it much harder to do what they wish could be done. In truth, competitors can be supporters of a company using Alpha learning.

We discovered that few categories start to grow significantly until there are several aggressive competitors active in the category. Until then, it's just a new idea without much traction. Once several competitors start pushing the benefits of the product or category of products, demand begins to grow geometrically. Unlike the traditional assumption that the number of competitors grows in proportion to the demand, we found just the opposite. It takes competitors to grow the category.

Before there is really enough demand to generate sufficient growth to sustain that many competitors, a new category needs multiple competitors who believe sufficiently in the potential of the new category to invest in it and make people aware of it. That early influx of competitors is why there is always a purging of competitors after a new category has started to grow significantly. Only those who created the greatest number of Supporting Alpha Assets (see Chapter 4) were able to survive; but it took the crowd to create the demand to drive the needed growth.

In a more established category, an Alpha uses the "following" behavior of competitors (described in Chapter 2) to create more demand for its own products and services. The more competitors try to compete against the Alpha's offering, the more they compare themselves to the Alpha's offering. This only helps prospective customers understand why the Alpha's product is so good. One of Wal-Mart's greatest assets is the resistance that is generated to their store entering a new market. After all, if Wal-Mart is so good that it puts smaller businesses out of business, then it must be the place to go.

Competitive emulation is also a benefit to the one being copied. It's not just a sign of respect but also a sign of desperation for the emulator. The company that has to come up with another version of the original is saying that the original was worth something. If the Alpha keeps its head and doesn't panic by falling into price promotion to overcome this competitive pressure, it can actually *increase* customer aspirations to buy its products or services through this competitive pressure.

The saddest part of competition is that more CEOs lose sleep over the thought that a competitor might undercut them and steal business away from them than they do about whether they are doing enough to create something worth following. The real concern should not be with those competitors who are trying to undercut you, but, rather, with a competitor that is driving new, higher-level expectations that draw customers away from aspiring to own your product.

Limiting the success of the undercutting competitor is accomplished by making it an unacceptable trade-off to buy their product rather than yours. By using a strategic innovation process based upon Alpha learning that drives expectations in higher-level emotional needs satisfaction while satisfying at least minimum functional needs, you continually make competitors a second choice to your product or service. This doesn't mean that they won't have business. But you will have the *best* business from the best and most profitable customers. This is an issue of profitability, price leverage, and strategic control more than it is of owning all the business in the category.

Even with technology breakthroughs that can be fairly easily copied, the same principle applies. Apple could not have been as successful with its iPod technology against many less-expensive competitors if it had not created higher-level emotional expectations of owning a real iPod rather than a cheaper competitor. Having a ready source of music through iTunes that could work only on an iPod MPEG player was a Supporting Alpha Asset, but it was not the critical one driving Apple's success. In fact, with a lesser brand, that strategy could have backfired and harmed sales rather than helped them.

If another competitor is the one that comes up with a breakthrough technology, what do you do? You use Alpha learning to do whatever you can to drive expectations to your product. Drive expectations in the areas of higher-level self-satisfaction and personal significance fulfillment. There have been many superior technologies that have not become standard. The DOS operating system was not as efficient as CPM. VHS videotape was not as good as Beta, which was not as good as video discs. But it wasn't the quality or effectiveness of the technology that won the day.

> *Your competitors can become your strongest marketing support system once you understand how The Alpha Factor works.*

The key to controlling competitors is to be clearly focused on addressing market segments that you want most to control, leaving competitors less-desirable segments to sell. Don't expect to take away all the business of a competitor. Like a cornered animal, the competitor will fight almost insanely to survive, harming itself and most of the category in the process. By leaving less-desirable segments available as "easy pickings" for competitors, you let them satisfy the less-profitable needs segments, allowing you to take the best there is.

The place to start is at The Alpha Factor website (*www .thealphafactor.com*), where you can find the tools to help you understand how to make your competitors your best supporting marketing assets.

# BIG AH-HA #9: DON'T FOLLOW THE LEADER.

*Non-Alpha thinking*: "Follow the leader, because he obviously knows what he's doing."

Strategic differentiation is critical to long-term, self-sustaining success. All too many companies seem to think that taking a cue from the dominant share leader of the category is a smart way to increase their own share and dominance. Nothing could be further from the truth.

As we discussed in Big Ah-ha #8, every time you follow the leader, you convince customers in your category that the

> *A follower can never be the controlling leader.*

leader's product is the one they should aspire to buy. Then, if you have not made yourself the low-price leader, you have made yourself redundant by the very fact that you are copying someone else's strategic appeal.

Just being different is not enough. The real trick is finding unmet higher-level needs that you can "own" as things you uniquely address well. These are the things that will create sustainable success and growth, and they will convince others to follow *your* lead.

A follower can never be the controlling leader.

There is no doubt that most marketers fail to differentiate themselves much from their competitors. They follow whatever looks like it might be working for someone else. That's a bad thing for everyone involved. It creates confusion in the marketplace. It creates downward price pressure. It creates a belief that price is the only real factor at work in customer buying decisions. It also tricks *real* leading brands into believing that they should not waste further efforts on trying to differentiate themselves and instead just slide back into the fray, as they think everyone else is doing.

Lack of differentiation is a plague that suffocates revenue generation; however, it is also the opportunity that opens the door for even weak potential Alphas to grow dramatically. In Chapter 2, we talked briefly about the packaged-cheese category at grocery stores. Kraft has the overwhelming share of the overall category of packaged cheeses, but they have been allowed to stay in that position only because there has been so little significant differentiation among competitors. Any cheese marketer that takes the time to address higher-level needs rather than just thinking they are selling cheese could grow significantly in this very crowded category.

The secret to successful differentiation is finding those higher-level needs that are unmet in any significant way and that you can address in a way that drives expectations higher. It takes creativity, but we proved that it works in even the toughest situations. Your only other choice is to blindly follow the leader and make yourself a survival or scavenger brand.

The Alpha Factor website (*www.thealphafactor.com*) is the fastest way to discover the path to leadership rather than just being another follower. There you will find all the tools you need to take control of competitors and make yourself the one to be followed.

BIG AH-HA #10: THE CUSTOMER DECISION PROCESS IS EXTREMELY COMPLEX, BUT IT CAN BE UNDERSTOOD, QUANTIFIED, AND INFLUENCED (WITHOUT JUST USING PRICE AS THE MOTIVATOR).

*Non-Alpha thinking*: "Customer decision processes are too inconsistent and too emotional to be measured, quantified, or influenced consistently."

Customer decision processes are complex and hard to follow at times. The process of understanding why customers make the decisions they do is hampered by incorrect information coming from normal information sources, a wrong model of what to look for, and the fact that customers often can't (or won't) tell you why they did what they did. Sales teams, distribution channels, employees, and all the other normal sources of market information that most companies use are not accurate sources—each has a bias and blindness that taints the insights you might gain from them. Traditional research measurements only help perpetuate wrong thinking about drivers of decisions. And customers are typically not introspective enough to readily know why they do what they do.

Price willing to pay = Perceived benefits + perceived pain to NOT

purchase − perceived pain to obtain it

Perceived benefits = (Self-satisfaction fulfillment + Personal

significance fulfillment)$^2$ * (perceived functional needs satisfaction +

perceived differentiation) * Communications Effectiveness

Once I discovered how to get customers to really verbalize, or discover for themselves, the actual processes they were using to make decisions, I was able to develop a formula that defines the buying process. In a simplified form, here is how people define the value or price they are willing to pay for a product:

Before a person decides how much something is worth to them, they go through an evaluation of what they perceive the benefits of buying the item might be. They add to that how painful it would be *not* to buy it. (That means, can they easily live without it?) And then they finally evaluate how much pain they think it is worth to purchase it. "Pain" includes how much they will pay, how far they will go to get it, how long they will wait, how easily they can get it to work, and other such considerations.

If what they see as the price on the product is higher than is justified by the results of that evaluation, they reevaluate, buy another product, or move on.

The real tricky part is in the evaluation of perceived benefits. As they evaluate perceived benefits, there is a good deal of competitive comparison that goes on. This is where they try to decide how much someone else is asking for benefits that they see as parallel to those of the product being considered.

What most people believe happens here is an evaluation of functional differentiation and perceived product performance. How well does the product meet needs and how different is that from competitive products? We discovered something quite different. Functional needs satisfaction (that is, product performance) and perceived differentiation are indeed important factors, but they are only a small part of the total evaluation. The effectiveness of marketing communications, such as packaging, advertising, merchandising, and sales support materials, plays a significant role, because it helps both educate and set expectations. Even more critical, however, is the fulfillment of self-satisfaction and personal significance. Where these two factors are addressed, their impact is squared. They can easily overcome product performance weaknesses, at least as long as minimum functional requirements are met. They can also overcome a lack of functional differentiation or poor marketing communications effectiveness in extreme cases.

> *Most companies work hard to increase "value" by building in more features, yet features are far less important than is emotional needs fulfillment.*

Most companies work hard to increase value for their products by building in more features, yet features are far less important to the value of your product than is emotional needs fulfillment.

The extraordinary importance of emotional needs fulfillment as a driver of value is the core of Alpha learning. It is even more integral to a company's success than the millions of dollars the company invests in product improvements or marketing communications each year. Both the product improvements and the marketing communications can only serve to support and prove the perceived emotional needs fulfillment anticipated.

The customer decision process is understandable, quantifiable, and capable of being influenced, if you forget the old models that have never worked and use Alpha learning to understand it.

Every tool discussed on The Alpha Factor website (*www .thealphafactor.com*) is based upon an understanding of how this formula plays out in real-world decisions. They are the same tools that were used to create the real-world successes discussed in this book.

## BIG AH-HA #11: YOU CAN MANAGE THE REVENUE SIDE OF THE PROFIT EQUATION.

*Non-Alpha thinking*: "Profit is driven by being the low-cost provider; revenue-side investments are a waste of money."

Here's a big surprise. You *can* control the revenue side by influencing the customer decision process and controlling your competitors. As this entire book demonstrates, customers make decisions more on the basis of emotional needs fulfillment than they do on the basis of functional needs satisfaction, or price, or availability, or any of the traditional factors that we have all been taught drive customer decisions. That emotional needs fulfillment can be controlled, managed, and improved to drive continuous improvements in profit outcomes.

Most CEOs believe that the revenue side is far too unpredictable to be controllable or manageable. The big surprise of the Alpha Factor Project was that we discovered you can have far greater control over your revenue generation than would normally be believed. It takes an understanding of what creates an Alpha and how you can use that learning to help yourself gain more control—even if you have no hope or aspiration to become the overall Alpha of your category.

Take strategic control over how you create and maintain *influence* in the marketplace, and you can create far more control over your future success than any cost controls have ever created. You can control your influence in the marketplace by purposefully driving the expectations of customers, referral agents, and your distribution network. Once you do that, you make competitors follow your lead, which not only strengthens you but verifies the expectations that you created. The result is that you now lead the category toward a future that *you* and your company are creating, not some competitor.

The big result is greater profitability. You have greater price leverage, meaning you can charge more for what you sell, and you don't have to use discounting as often or as aggressively as your competitors have to do to generate demand. You also facilitate the ability to create future profitability every time you use Alpha learning rather than falling into traditional tactical approaches.

> *You can control your influence in the marketplace by purposefully driving customer expectations.*

You can control and manage the revenue side by using Alpha tools much as you can better manage the cost side using Six Sigma tools. Start with a visit to The Alpha Factor website (*www .thealphafactor.com*), and discover how you can take control of your company's revenue generation in ways you never imagined possible in the past.

## BIG AH-HA #12: DRAMATIC SHIFTS IN MARKET SHARE CAN OCCUR WITHIN SHORT TIME PERIODS, EVEN IN WELL-ESTABLISHED AND HIGHLY COMPETITIVE CATEGORIES.

*Non-Alpha thinking*: "Gradual, incremental growth is what must be expected."

Most corporate executives find it hard to believe that dramatic, revolutionary growth can occur for a company that has been stagnant for many years. The fact that this growth can occur in a short period of time and be sustainable without the use of discounting may be beyond anything they have seen before. Not only is it possible, but it is also *probable* that a company will experience dramatic growth when using Alpha learning to drive it.

> *In every case . . . the growth happened in short periods of time . . . usually within a year or less.*

As I have described in this book, throughout this entire project it was commonplace to discover ways to create growth that turned around long-term stagnation or decline. We were also able to take top-performing companies in their category and help them find ways to create even more growth using existing capabilities and resources. And in every case where the opportunities identified were pursued, the growth happened in a short period of time—usually within a year or less.

In cases where growth was undermined or slowed after it had started, it was either because corporate management *wanted* the growth to slow down or because they fell back into old tactical methods of discounting, promotion, or following competitors.

Using Alpha learning, it is possible to create dramatic growth in unbelievably short periods of time without falling into self-destructive tactics like discounting. That growth is controllable, if the company is prepared to control it and is willing to believe that it is possible.

Don't be fooled into believing that profitable change has to occur slowly. By using the Alpha Factor tools you'll find at The Alpha Factor website (*www.thealphafactor.com*), you can create sustainable, profitable change in less time than you ever imagined.

---

## BIG AH-HA #13: YOU CAN CREATE A PROCESS FOR GENERATING SELF-SUSTAINING SUCCESS.

---

*Non-Alpha thinking*: "Sustainable success is not possible."

Sustainable success is possible. It doesn't have to be a constant roller coaster of innovate, stagnate, innovate, stagnate, as many companies experience. In fact, we discovered that when Alpha learning is used as the model for innovation, it's hard to kill the success you created, even when competitors try to kill it.

Sustainable growth is not driven from within but from outside your company. It comes from having a purposeful strategic approach to tracking expectations and then continually driving expectations to new and higher levels of emotional needs satisfaction. Where innovation falls flat is when it is more intently focused on creating new functionality without correlating emotional satisfaction. The thing that kills growth is not inevitability, but, rather, people

> *It's hard to kill the success you create using Alpha learning, even when competitors try hard to do so.*

who either give up on the things that created success for their company or decided to change directions without understanding what the Alpha Assets were that needed to be protected in the midst of change. (See Chapter 4.)

Sears could still be the largest and most dominant retailer in the world. It wasn't Kmart's or even Wal-Mart's prices that killed Sears; it was Sears' management losing sight of what had made that retailer great and then giving over the company to outsiders who had no idea what Sears was or had been.

Ford and Chevrolet could still be the powerhouses of middle-class automobiles. It wasn't the Japanese automakers that killed Ford and Chevrolet; it was their own blindness to what customers really wanted and would pay for.

It also isn't big technological innovations that drive new trends in markets; it is changes in customer expectations that drive big trends. Intel hasn't made itself the Alpha in microprocessors by just offering new technology. AMD actually had a better-performing processor at a lower cost to consumers when it first started marketing Intel's product again. Intel has been smart enough to drive expectations for faster and faster processing, while making itself the *perceived* innovation leader. Intel has even gone as far as to contract software developers to create software that requires more memory and more processing power just to drive continual demand for faster and more potent processing power. It has gone even further, to make "Intel Inside" an important emotional sales feature of a computer, nullifying the hard work that AMD and others tried to do to make lower-priced and faster processors available.

FedEx almost didn't make it, because it took them so long to drive customer expectations to demand overnight delivery. They had to have multiple new infusions of capital before customer expectations were finally generated that drove that demand. Now everyone competes to prove that they deliver as fast as FedEx, but for lower cost. The only way FedEx will fall from its top position is if it gives that position away.

Coca-Cola would not have survived their mistake of dropping their original formula for New Coke in the 1980s if it weren't for the loyalty and expectations their customers had developed over decades. Nor would John Deere have survived introducing a low-priced, mass-merchandiser line of Sabre tractors that almost killed their dealer relationships and customer confidence in the company. Their success was driven by customers who made sure the company survived and prospered even after serious mistakes.

The point is that if you have a purposeful strategic innovation process that is focused on driving new, higher-level expectations, then you can drive sustainable success. It is only when those managing the process give up or allow themselves to believe that someone else has the better solution to the problem that the success falters.

All of the innovation tools you will find at The Alpha Factor website (*www.thealphafactor.com*) are designed to create innovations that drive greater control, which in turn drives more innovation by pushing new, higher-level expectations that you control. The result is that you control category decisions, until you give up and allow someone else to take that control.

## BIG AH-HA #14: INNOVATION HAS TO BE MORE THAN NEW PRODUCT DEVELOPMENT OR IMPROVED INTERNAL PROCESSES.

*Non-Alpha thinking*: "You need breakthrough products or breakthroughs in pricing or quality to create big growth."

We were continually amazed at how much growth could be created simply by using Alpha learning instead of relying on big breakthroughs to create positive change. We've also discussed how the quality movement has not generated the growth that it was purported to create. Growth is actually created less by new products, new processes, or more efficient ways of doing things; it is created by using the basic principles of Alpha learning to get your competitors and distributors to follow your lead, and that puts you in firmer control of your future than any new product can accomplish.

Sure, we uncovered opportunities for several new products among our test companies. These products were even helpful in generating the growth they experienced, but those products were not the key to that growth. They were instead just *one* of the means used to support a general movement toward addressing higher-level emotional needs and to thereby change category expectations. In most companies, no new products were used to create growth, and yet those companies typically experienced growth in excess of 25 percent.

Assuming that you need a big breakthrough is just one more way to convince yourself that you can't grow, so why even try? Instead, you fall back on self-destructive pricing and other tactical methods that undermine your ability to grow in the future.

> *Assuming that you need a big innovation breakthrough is just one more way to convince yourself that you can't grow.*

Changing the corporate mind set, however, is not all that easy. Making the change from reacting to customer or distributor demand, which seldom correlates to their actual needs or desires, to driving customer and distributor expectations requires a vision for a new process of evaluating market opportunities. That's why the Alpha Factor Project was so important. It helped prove that another way of addressing the market could create far more profit, far more growth, far more of just about everything a company wants, using fewer resources to accomplish that growth than any of the traditional methods have done.

Innovation must incorporate the process of driving new expectations, especially higher-level ones, or it will not be sustainable, and it cannot generate significant new growth. This has always been the problem with incremental innovation. It typically looks only at slightly improving existing offerings in the category. Real, sustainable results are driven by innovation that pushes expectations among customers, referral agents, and your distribution network higher and higher, giving you control over the future of the category.

Every tool you will find on The Alpha Factor website (*www.thealphafactor.com*) focuses innovation upon both product innovation *and* creating new expectations that drive greater long-term dominance.

# THE FINAL CHAPTER: YOUR NEXT STEPS

Want to use what we learned through the Alpha Factor Project to make your company stronger, more resilient, and more in control of your future? It won't happen by waiting until you have everyone in your company convinced or prepared. Make a commitment today to start testing Alpha learning wherever and whenever you can. You will be stunned at the results, if you truly follow through on it and do not allow yourself or others to undermine the process with the old, traditional self-destructive tactics.

My first real experiment with my early hypotheses happened while I was responsible for the growth of one small segment of business at a Fortune 500 company. I was able to cut promotional costs by half and grow sales by between 6 percent and 220 percent in 19 district sales offices. It did not shake up the entire company, but it was enough to get attention and make others try to figure out what I had done that was different. That led to other efforts to change our approach to the market. Your first steps don't have to be big ones; you just have to take the first steps.

> *Any company that doesn't undermine its own efforts can grow dramatically using Alpha learning.*

Start by finding a way to believe in yourself and your company. We discovered that self-doubt is the biggest hurdle to success with Alpha learning. Based on the results of our tests and research, I believe that any company that doesn't undermine its own efforts can grow dramatically using Alpha learning. We proved it even with companies that had not grown in more than a decade. Stop listening to the salespeople and distributors, or even to customers who continually try to make you believe that you are overpriced. Instead, show them that by changing expectations, you suddenly go from the perception of being overpriced to that of being underpriced without changing your price at all. A good place to start discovering your real potential could be The Alpha Factor website, where you will find not only tools to help you discover how you can take a leading role in your category, but you will also find much more information about the Alpha Model.

Teach every employee to start listening for hints about higher-level emotional needs (self-satisfaction and personal significance) that are not being satisfied either by your company or by anyone else in your category. I'm not talking about customer satisfaction. I'm talking about understanding what the *real* motivations are behind a person's behavior that goes beyond what is being said directly. Don't let a single conversation go by without seeking out what it is that person really *wishes* he could get, rather than just settling for the superficial needs he finds it safe enough to verbalize.

Create a new process for assessing your company's real Alpha Assets. Using the filter of Alpha learning, they will certainly be far different from the list of strengths you currently believe are driving your company's success. Understand what your Core Alpha Asset is (see Chapter 4). Make a comprehensive list of your Supporting Alpha Assets, and understand which of them are critical to supporting your Core Alpha Asset's growth potential.

> *Look beyond what is being addressed today by competitors or how things are currently being done.*

Don't be afraid to look far beyond what is being addressed today by competitors in your category or the way things are being done now. When one of our test company CEOs realized that he had been wasting millions of dollars every year on things that were only hurting his future growth potential, he was livid with himself. He had not realized that he did not have to play the game by the rules that had been set for him. In fact, by breaking those rules and creating new expectations, he generated many hundreds of millions of dollars in new profit for his company. People have an insatiable appetite for having their higher-level needs addressed. You can always keep upping the ante and addressing more of them. Plan to satisfy at least minimal functional needs, but push to satisfy maximum emotional and ego satisfaction needs.

Be brutal in assessing your weaknesses. Don't blind yourself to those weaknesses just because you believe you can't change them or they are "not that bad." If you spot something that doesn't support your Core Alpha Asset and is not helpful in moving you from a cost-based, price-based view of revenue generation to an expectation-driving view, then get rid of it or change it.

Don't be put off because you don't believe you can ever become the overall Alpha of your category. We proved that almost every company has the potential to create more growth, more profit, and more control over its own future by using Alpha learning to drive strategic planning, implementation, and measurement. Become the Alpha of your own subsegment and reap the benefits. Make every competitor that even knows you are there start following your lead, and watch both your profit and your control grow.

Don't give up. You will hear lots of contrary voices among your staff, who don't want to believe that they have invested their careers in a self-destructive model. The best proof is your own new success. Use Alpha learning, and let the proof talk for you. Yes, the successes generated by using Alpha learning can be undermined. I've seen that happen all too often. But if you fairly use this model and track results, they will speak for themselves.

> *Almost every company has the potential to create more growth, more profit, and more control over its own future by using Alpha learning.*

The Alpha Factor Project finally answered the question of what actually creates long-term sustainable success by stripping away the hype that has clouded this subject for so long. It took a long time to discover the answer and equally as long to prove that it could create success, but it succeeded.

Now it's your turn to start leading the pack instead of following someone else's lead. Take a new look at your business and discover that you can make your company the one that everyone else follows, giving you control over your own future growth and that of others.

# ABOUT THE AUTHOR

Wes Ball has been a strategic innovation consultant and business owner for 25 years. After 10 years as an executive in two Fortune 500 corporations, he founded The Ball Group, a marketing research and strategic consulting firm. Wes has worked with top executive teams in more than 75 companies to help them discover and address new strategic growth opportunities. He has worked with companies ranging in size from the Fortune 100 to midsized companies to smaller regional businesses to start-ups.

As a management coach, Wes has also been able to help top executive teams align internal resources to drive self-sustaining growth and to create a corporate culture that continually drives customer expectations.

Wes can be reached at w.ball@ballgroup.com.

You can learn even more about the Alpha Factor and how you can use this learning for your company by visiting The Alpha Factor website at www.thealphafactor.com.

# Index

## A

Alpha Assets v, 83-89, 91-93, 95, 97, 99, 101, 103, 105-115, 121-123, 125, 127, 129, 130, 132, 145, 150, 160, 168, 172, 180, 196, 204

AMD 196, 197

AMF 99

Apple 68, 69, 181, 182

Armstrong World Industries 7, 71, 73, 93-95, 101, 109, 162, 163

aspiring brand 20, 89, 101, 130

automakers 41, 132, 133, 138, 139, 140, 165, 196

## B

Basic Buying 24, 162

Ben & Jerry's 27, 28, 33, 40, 42, 43, 71, 73, 99, 109, 131, 140, 153, 157

Blackberry 69

Brand Central 51, 96

Breyers 28, 33, 42, 71, 153

## C

Caterpillar 71

Celotex 87, 101

chaos 3

Christian Dior 157

Classic Coke 70, 79, 129

Cobra 64

Coca-Cola 12, 19, 20, 70, 73, 79, 96, 97, 101, 109, 110, 120, 129, 197

Colgate-Palmolive 160

Core Alpha Assets 91, 92, 97, 105, 123, 132, 168

Craftsman tools 51, 95, 166

Cub Cadet 72

## D

Dom Perignon 157

drivers of decisions 50, 51, 55, 70, 74-78, 80, 82, 114, 123, 171, 175-178, 187

Duesenberg 71

# E

Easy Saver 103

Edy's/Dreyer's 28, 33, 153

Ethan Allen 157

Etiene Aignier 157

expectations 4-7, 17, 18, 21-24, 26, 28, 33, 34, 37, 41, 43, 49, 54, 55, 67, 73, 75, 76, 78, 80, 82, 84, 85, 88, 90, 91, 99, 115, 119, 120, 122-124, 127, 129-136, 138-140, 142, 148-150, 153, 154, 167, 169, 171, 173, 174, 177, 181, 182, 185, 189, 192, 195-198, 200, 201, 203, 205, 207

# F

FedEx 197

Ferrari 157

First Union Bank 169

food 6, 16, 23, 25, 26, 29, 31, 39, 120, 124, 146

Frederick's of Hollywood 100, 161

# G

GE 118

Godiva Chocolate 157

Good Humor 71

Good, Better, Best 162

# H

Häagen Dazs 157

Harley-Davidson 12, 49, 53, 90-92, 99, 107-110, 120, 129, 161, 164

Harvesting 111-114

Howard Johnson 71

# I

IBM 161

ice cream 27, 28, 33, 34, 42, 43, 73, 97-99, 124, 131, 140-142, 153, 154

innovation vii, 11, 13, 23-25, 38, 41, 42, 78, 81, 84, 118, 124, 131, 149, 154, 164, 177, 181, 195-201, 207

Intel 40, 41, 196

iPhone 68, 69

iPod 68, 181, 182

# J

John Deere 72, 129, 197

## K

Kenmore 95

Kmart 71, 96, 101, 121, 122, 142, 165, 196

Kraft 21, 22, 185

## L

L.L. Bean 165, 166

## M

Maslow, Abraham 61

Maslow's hierarchy of needs 61

McDonald's 49, 120

Measuring outcomes 125, 126

Microsoft 40, 66, 67, 149, 161

Montgomery Ward 100

motorcycles 49, 53, 91,92, 99, 107, 120, 129, 161, 164

Mustang 64

## N

Needs Satisfaction 22, 105, 106, 119-121, 123, 139, 141, 148, 160, 169, 172, 181, 188, 189, 191, 195

New Coke 20, 70, 97, 110, 19

## P

packaged-goods 160

Pepsi 20, 70, 73, 79, 101, 110, 120, 129

Porsche 157

price vi, ix, 8, 10-14, 21, 22, 24, 33, 34, 36-38, 40, 41, 43, 48, 52, 54-57, 59, 60, 68-71, 73, 75-78, 80, 84, 86-89, 96-99, 106, 109, 110, 119, 121, 122, 124, 127, 130-32, 134, 139, 154, 156-159, 162, 164, 168, 173, 176, 180, 181, 184, 185, 187, 188, 191, 192, 203, 205

## Q

quality vi, 20, 24, 48,-50, 52-54, 58, 64, 65, 68, 71, 72, 78, 81, 84, 86-88, 91, 94, 95, 99, 106, 107, 115, 122, 132, 137, 139, 164-166, 182, 199

quick-serve restaurants 59

## R

retailing 24, 25, 53, 55, 100

Rolex 157

## S

Sabre tractors 197

Satisfaction Guaranteed or Your Money Back 51

scavenger brand 101, 124,128, 186

Sears 24, 25, 50-55, 71, 73, 95, 96, 100, 101, 121, 129, 130, 142, 161, 162, 166, 196

Six Sigma 118, 164, 192

Snapple 71

Softsoap 71, 160

Starbucks iii, 12, 160, 161

structure to the category 33

Subway Sandwiches and Salads 6, 59

Supporting Alpha Assets 89, 105-115, 121, 123, 125, 127, 129, 130, 145, 160, 172, 180, 204

survival brand 20, 115, 130

## T

Tiffany's 157

TQM (Total Quality Management) 164

## U

U.S. Department of the Treasury 5, 6, 102, 103,170

U.S. Savings Bonds 5, 6, 101, 102, 103, 146, 170

## V

value 9, 12, 13, 30, 31, 33, 60, 70, 86, 96, 107, 109-115, 122, 133, 156, 157, 159, 165, 166, 176-178, 188,-190

Victoria's Secret 40, 73, 86, 100, 107, 109, 110, 157, 161

## W

Wachovia Bank 169

Wal-Mart 55, 56, 96, 107, 110, 121, 142, 165, 180, 196

Woolworth 71